Stanley Roamer, Henry Edward Manning

Cardinal Manning as presented in his own Letters and Notes

Stanley Roamer, Henry Edward Manning

Cardinal Manning as presented in his own Letters and Notes

ISBN/EAN: 9783743336384

Manufactured in Europe, USA, Canada, Australia, Japa

Cover: Foto ©ninafisch / pixelio.de

Manufactured and distributed by brebook publishing software (www.brebook.com)

Stanley Roamer, Henry Edward Manning

Cardinal Manning as presented in his own Letters and Notes

CARDINAL MANNING

AS PRESENTED IN HIS OWN LETTERS AND NOTES.

BY

STANLEY ROAMER.

LONDON:
ELLIOT STOCK, 62, PATERNOSTER ROW, E.C.
1896.

INTRODUCTION.

IN a matter of controversy we very seldom get plain statements, and in a religious controversy, we may almost say never.

In the recently published 'Life of Cardinal Manning,' on the other hand, we have Letters, Diaries, Journals, and Autobiographical Notes, as to the authenticity of which there can be no dispute.

Mr. Purcell tells us in his preface (p. vi):

'All his Diaries, Journals, and Autobiographical Notes, in accordance with his wish and will, passed into my possession. I did not attempt to revise or reverse Cardinal Manning's directions. In his Diaries, Journals, and Notes he told the story of his own life, laid bare the workings of his heart; its trials and temptations, sometimes its secrets and sorrows. It was not for me by suppressions to amend or to blur his handiwork.'

Mr. Purcell is a Roman Catholic himself; was an

intimate friend of Cardinal Manning's, and went through with Cardinal Manning, during his lifetime, nearly all these Diaries, Journals, Letters, and Notes. Mr. Purcell has, since the Cardinal's death, had an opportunity of consulting many of the late Cardinal's personal friends, and has thus been enabled to throw additional light on many points.

We have almost wholly confined ourselves to Roman Catholic authors in dealing with any controversial matter; but it must be borne in mind that in all strictures that may be passed on any opinions, motives, or events, that are related in the Life, we are not judging the man, but the ecclesiastical system that lends itself to the successful issue of such motives or opinions. Cardinal Manning's object in compiling this record of his life, and in causing it to be published during the lifetime of many alluded to in these Diaries, Journals, and Notes, may be apparent by the time we have reached the closing years of his career.

CHAPTER I.

IT must not be forgotten that, as Mr. Purcell tells us, numerous excisions have been made in the Diaries, and masses of letters have been destroyed, so that in these volumes we view the Cardinal as he wished to be seen.

Mr. Purcell is perfectly straightforward in his comments and criticisms on matters appearing in the letters or Diaries; but his conclusions are in some cases drawn from a strictly Roman Catholic point of view, and would not, therefore, appeal to those who do not hold the Roman Catholic faith.

There seems some doubt as to the date of the late Cardinal's birth. Mr. Purcell gives it as having taken place on July 15, 1807, but others, including the Cardinal himself in a recorded conversation, state the correct date to be July 15, 1808. The date of baptism, at least, is known beyond any doubt whatever, and that was May 25, 1809, and the delay is thus accounted for by Mr. Purcell: 'Mr. William Manning, in those days at the height of his prosperity, was not a little prone to ostentation; and his ambition was not satisfied, apparently, unless he had a Bishop to baptize his children. The convenience of so important a personage had, of course, to be studied, and that may account for the delay.'[1]

As an illustration of this proneness to ostentation, Mr. Purcell gives a note to the following effect:

'W. Manning was in the habit of driving every morning from Totteridge to the City, a distance of eight miles, in a coach and four.'[2]

We may compare this with Manning's own account of his father in the House of Commons. It will afford a good instance of Manning's peculiar way of viewing things.

'But he was too refined, modest and sensitive to make a display, or to overdo anything. He was in danger of underdoing what he did from fear of display.'[3]

We shall frequently find this 'sensitiveness' applied to Manning's own character, but we must leave our readers to judge of its appropriateness.

In due course Manning went to Harrow School, and of that period Bishop Oxenden gives the following anecdote:

'There was even in those early days a little self-assertion in his character. On one occasion he was invited to dinner at Mr. Cunningham's, the Vicar of

---

[1] Vol. i., p. 3. [2] Vol. i., p. 3, note. [3] Vol. i., p. 8.

the parish. On his return at night, one of his friends questioned him as to whom he had met, whether he had enjoyed his evening, and especially as to what part he had taken in the general conversation. To these inquiries he answered that he had spent the evening pleasantly enough, but that he had said little, and, indeed, had been almost silent, for there were two or three superior persons present; and he added, " You know that my motto is 'Aut Cæsar aut nullus.' I therefore held my tongue and listened."[1]

Manning proceeded to Oxford, and Mr. Purcell tells us that 'On March 12, 1829, an undergraduate, young in years if not in audacity, rose to speak for the first time at the Union at Oxford. . . . He rose, as the veteran orator without a blush once confessed, in fear and trembling to speak his first speech.'[2]

The comment on this and the accompanying anecdote shows one great characteristic of the man throughout his life : ' After this event, in a life destined to be so eventful and so full of surprises, it was noted by his contemporaries that Manning ever wore a look of self consciousness; he seemed to fancy, as he walked through the halls and corridors, or sat in the common-room, that every eye regarded him either with admiration or in envy. It was said in jest in those days, that Manning was self-conscious even in his nightcap.'[3]

At times Mr. Purcell's conclusions as to his character

---

[1] Vol. i., p. 27. [2] Vol. i., p. 29. [3] Vol. i., p. 30.

seem somewhat contradictory, but, as we proceed, many of these seeming contradictions will disappear. The two following extracts hardly appear to allude to the same man: 'Manning, it must be confessed, joined the Union at a lucky moment. Samuel Wilberforce had just quitted Oxford, and Gladstone had not as yet arrived. . . . Manning was equal to the occasion; he combined ambition and boldness with considerable tact and a conciliatory manner. He from the beginning was not one to hide his light under a bushel.'[1] And, in allusion to the Harrow dinner: 'He was, although it has not been pointed out or perhaps discovered by his critics, very shy by nature, and unwilling to commit himself before strangers. It was only by long habit and strength of will that he succeeded in overcoming and concealing his natural shyness and timidity.'[2]

'He from the beginning was not one to hide his light under a bushel' does not quite tally with 'natural shyness and timidity'; nor does it at all agree with the Harrow dinner story and the 'Aut Cæsar aut nullus'; nor yet, again, does 'as the veteran orator without a blush once confessed,' for a first attempt at public speaking, show the 'natural shyness and timidity.' And it is idle to pretend that the self-assertion at Harrow or at Oxford was produced by 'long habit and strength of will.'

[1] Vol. i., p. 34.   [2] Vol. i., p. 28.

We shall find numberless instances of his 'unwillingness to commit himself before strangers,' and friends, too, and even those on a most intimate footing; but that peculiarity is fully accounted for by his usual practice of 'seeing how the land lay' before taking any course or adopting any opinion.

Manning himself gives us an autobiographical note relating to this period, in which we see his first views as to entering the Church:

'After this I spoke from time to time, and became interested in politics, and made acquaintance with men going on into public life, and my whole mind was drawn that way. . . . I had always disliked the thought of being a clergyman, and this political aspiration finished.'[1]

'Politics' is a most comprehensive word. In times now, happily, long past, in England at least, ecclesiastical politics were paramount. The ecclesiastic was supreme in State, as in Church. Had Cardinal Manning lived a couple of centuries earlier, he might have combined his political aspirations with his ecclesiastical functions, and with considerable success, as he was unrivalled in concealing his real intentions and thoughts, and could deceive his most intimate friends on the most vital points of ecclesiastical politics. But his political aspirations, so far as regarded his becoming a Member of Parliament, were nipped in the bud by his father's bankruptcy.

[1] Vol. i., p. 30, note.

The following statement by the late Lord Forester, Dean of York, appeared in the *Times* on January 20, 1892, six days after Cardinal Manning's death :

'Henry Manning was a schoolfellow of Miss Bevan's brother Robert, and was wont to spend the greater part of his holidays at Trent Park. She told me they were as brother and sister, "so much so that, if he were to come into this room now, I should talk to him like my brother." His great desire was to enter Parliament, but, his father having lost all his property, his prospects in that direction were dashed to the ground. His chief failing in those days was excessive ambition. After his father's losses, which changed his whole career, when he next came to Trent she perceived how depressed he was ; in their walks together she endeavoured to cheer him, telling him there were higher aims still that he had not thought of. "What are they?" She replied, "The kingdom of heaven ; heavenly ambitions are not closed against you." He listened, and said in reply he did not know but she was right. She suggested reading the Bible together, saying she was sure her brother Robert would join them. This they did during the whole of that vacation, every morning after breakfast. It was her conviction that this was the beginning of Henry Manning's religious life. He always used to speak of her as his spiritual mother. When the time came for him and her brother Robert to return to

Oxford, she proposed that they should continue reading the same portions together—he and her brother at Oxford, and she at Trent—and they were to correspond on the subjects. The result was that she had piles of his letters. After his change of faith, and when she was living at Broseley, he wrote to her, asking her to return him his letters, as he said they might compromise him.'

These letters are, of course, among those which have been destroyed.

In 'Notes and Reminiscences' of Oxford life, written a few years before his death, Cardinal Manning states: 'During my time at Oxford a religious change had come over me. First, the daily chapel became very soothing, especially the Psalms and lessons. . . . And yet the thought of being a clergyman had so utterly passed from me, that I wrote to my father and told him that it was impossible.'[1]

The 'spiritual mother' is here entirely ignored. But the ambitious man, if successful, proverbially kicks away the ladder on which he has risen, and we shall not find Manning wanting in this respect.

His letters to his brother-in-law, John Anderdon, who was his most intimate friend and confidant from boyhood, and who was set to work the oracle to get whatever was required from his father, although they, as Mr. Purcell tells us, 'in their fulness and freedom

[1] Vol. i., p. 67.

give a graphic picture of Manning's mind at the time, contain no reference to the subject of religion, or to the Church of England, or to ecclesiastical questions.'[1]

In 1831 he obtained a supernumerary clerkship at the Colonial Office, his duties only obliging him to attend at the office when his services were required. He had a considerable amount of spare time on his hands, and utilized it on one occasion to 'pursue an active canvass of the resident Fellows of Merton for a vacant Fellowship. But he was confronted with the primary objection that he was not in Orders; for, though unmarried laymen are eligible, clergymen are preferred.'[2]

In an autobiographical note, written more than half a century after taking Orders, Cardinal Manning says:

'At this time I came to know Henry Blunt, of Chelsea, and found him not only earnest, but highly intelligent. He had been, I think, twelfth or fourteenth wrangler. All this made a new thought spring up in me—not to be a clergyman in the sense of my old destiny, but to give up the world and to live for God and for souls. This grew on me daily. I had been long praying much, and going habitually to churches. It was a turning-point in my life. I wrote and asked Henry Blunt to come to me at the Colonial Office. He did so; and after a long weighing of the case, I resolved to resign, and to give myself to the

---

[1] Vol. i., p. 65.　　　　[2] Vol. i., p. 72.

service of God and of souls. My doubt was whether God had called me; and I had a great fear of going uncalled. It was as purely a call from God as all He has given me since. It was a call *ad veritatem et ad seipsum*. As such I tested it and followed it.'[1]

In a further autobiographical note Cardinal Manning states: 'In a day or two I saw Lord Goderich[2] and resigned; but the giving up of political life was an enormous wrench to me.... Moreover, the thought of being a clergyman was positively repulsive to me. I had an intense recoil from the secularity of the Established Church. I can say, as before God, that I had not a spark of ecclesiastical ambition. The sight of an apron and of a shovel hat literally provoked me. The title "Father in God," applied to Bishops living in ease, irritated me.'[3]

Manning wrote to his brother-in-law, John Anderdon, under date 'Oxford, March 9, 1832— . . . I think the whole step has been too precipitate. I have rather allowed the instance of my friends and the allurements of an agreeable curacy in many respects to get the better of my sober judgment.'[4]

No one can have the least doubt as to whether the letter written at the time to his brother-in-law, or the

[1] Vol. i., p. 93.
[2] The head of the Colonial Office, then merged in the War Office.
[3] Vol. i., p. 96.   [4] Vol. i., p. 88.

autobiographical note written fifty years later, correctly represented the state of Manning's feelings at the time of the renunciation of political life. As Mr. Purcell very pointedly suggests: 'In his "Reminiscences," written late in life, Cardinal Manning seems to have "caught on" to the idea that in resigning his clerkship in the Colonial Office he was giving up "political life," whereas in reality he was only giving up the Civil Service. For the Colonial Office is no more a school for politics than the Foreign Office, or Somerset House, or the Post-Office. His chance of entering into political life was lost by his father's bankruptcy in 1831.'[1]

With regard to the dislike of apron and shovel hat and the title 'Father in God,' Mr. Gladstone says: 'Manning was always most loyal to the Church, and spoke of its Bishops with great reverence.'[2]

Manning entered on his duties as curate at Lavington, Sussex, on January 3, 1833, under the Rev. John Sargent, who was also Rector of Graffham. The Rev. John Sargent died from consumption on May 3, 1833, soon after which date Manning became engaged to Miss Caroline Sargent, and was presented to the living by her grandmother, Mrs. Sargent. On November 7, 1833, Manning was married. On taking Orders, Manning again canvassed his friends about

[1] Vol. i., p. 105, note.   [2] Vol. i., p. 97.

the Merton Fellowship, and was duly elected. In July, 1837, Manning's wife died, and Mr. Purcell quotes Manning's lifelong friend, Mr. Richmond, R.A., as saying: 'His grief was great and abiding—too great for words; he never spoke of her. I was a frequent visitor in those days of sorrow, and often found Manning seated at the graveside of his wife, composing his sermons.'[1]

Against this we must put an entry in Manning's Diary, 1844-47. Among 'God's Ten Special Mercies' is to be found the date '1837.'[2]

Mr. Purcell's comments are somewhat unkind: 'By this marriage the designs of Providence in regard to the future Cardinal of the Holy Roman Church seemed to have been frustrated. But Providence has a long arm, and God in His wisdom took to Himself in the fourth year of her marriage the wife of Henry Edward Manning, the Cardinal-priest to be.'[3]

But Manning had given Mr. Purcell full cause for viewing the matter in this light, having told him that he had 'received a letter from the churchwardens, announcing that the grave at Lavington was falling into decay, and asking for instructions about putting it and keeping it in repair. "My reply was: It is best so; let it be. Time effaces all things."'[4]

[1] Vol. i., p. 123, note.
[2] Vol. i., p. 104, note.
[3] Vol. i., p. 104.
[4] Vol. i., p. 124.

And again: 'On his death in 1880, Frederick Manning bequeathed to his brother Henry two volumes of his letters, extending over a period of twenty years, from 1830 to 1850, but Cardinal Manning's ruthless scissors destroyed all the letters, 1833 to 1837, covering the interesting period of his married life.'[1]

No unprejudiced person can look with anything but disgust at this part of the story. Manning's 'self-consciousness' appeared again in the sitting by the graveside composing sermons, but we shall find this quality, or, as it is sometimes called, 'sensitiveness,' a conspicuous feature of Manning's character. He was a past-master in the art of posing.

Manning's wife and all her family were strong Evangelicals, and so was he himself, as Mr. Gladstone tells us: 'I met Manning by accident. It was on the occasion of a great meeting in 1835 or 1836, I think, called by Archbishop Howley in connection with the Christian Knowledge Society. I asked Manning what had brought him, a country clergyman, up to town. "To defend," was his answer, "the Evangelical cause against the attempts of the Archbishop." This shows that Manning belonged at that time to the section of the extreme Evangelicals.'[2]

But Mr. Purcell states: 'I am quoting these letters (Manning to Newman, and Newman to Man-

[1] Vol. i., p. 104, note.   [2] Vol. i., p. 116.

ning), not so much on account of their intrinsic interest, as to show Manning's friendly relations at the time (September, 1836) with Newman; and how, before he had as yet publicly broken with the Evangelical party, he was imbibing the principles of Tractarianism at the fountain-head.'[1]

And again: 'In 1837 Manning made, if I may so call it, a profession of faith in Newman and Pusey, the joint leaders at that time of the Tractarian movement.'[2]

We can easily understand this change. Manning's 'shyness' was coming into play, and he was 'not committing himself before strangers' as yet. Mr. Purcell tells us that in 1838 'favouring circumstances helped the young Rector of Lavington onwards and upwards. He was quick in discerning that the Tractarian movement was becoming a power in the land.'[3]

The creation of the Ecclesiastical Commission in 1838 roused immense feeling among all parties in the Church, and brought them into line against the Government, and on June 13 in that year Manning preached his sermon entitled 'Rule of Faith,' at the first visitation of Otter, the new Bishop of Chichester. By this sermon Manning 'gained the confidence and esteem of the Tractarian leaders, and was even invited by Newman to write for the *British Critic.*'[4]

[1] Vol. i., p. 226.
[2] Vol. i., p. 226.
[3] Vol. i., p. 128.
[4] Vol. i., p. 129.

Manning was ever keen to see 'how the land lay,' and Mr. Purcell explains :

'To free the Church of England from the bondage of the State was the desire of his heart, the end and aim of all his public labours. If the motive which aroused Bishop Otter and his episcopal brethren to action was love for the temporalities of the Church, Manning was inspired by the far higher and purer motive of safeguarding its spiritualities. Another advantage then had presented itself, another opportunity which he was quick to make use of : in opposing the Ecclesiastical Commission he was on the one hand following the lead of Newman, and co-operating with the Tractarian party at Oxford ; whilst on the other he was carrying out the work on which his own Bishop had set his heart, and acting in common with almost all the Bishops and dignitaries of the Church. It was an uncommon event, and a happy omen, to be spoken well of by the *British Critic* at Oxford, and to receive in London the benign blessings of the *Record*.'[1]

It is, at least, curious to find such a temporiser alluded to as the one individual who approached the subject with a 'purer and higher' motive than the numberless others who looked on the proposed change as almost a revolution.

Manning had not yet publicly professed himself

[1] Vol. i., p. 141.

a member of the Tractarian party. Of this we may be sure, that, if he had been known as a member of that party, the *Record* would not, in those times of extreme tension, have blessed him.

We have a further proof in an anecdote related by Mr. Purcell: 'The tact, temper of mind, and conciliatory manner which enabled Manning to win his way so early among men of the most opposite religious schools. from the Low Churchman who ruled at Chichester to the Tractarians of Oxford, may perhaps be exemplified in the most effectual manner by showing the mode and method of his dealing with the Archdeacon of Lewes. Archdeacon Hare was from beginning to end a staunch Low Churchman. Manning in a letter to him, dated September 17, 1840, wrote: "I wish I could have a book-talk with you. As a step towards it, send me the names of some theological works which you think true in principle and reasoning." It was, at any rate, modest in a disciple of Newman's, and a writer in the *British Critic*, to seek theological counsel from an Evangelical Archdeacon.'[1]

To an ordinary individual such conduct would not come under the head of 'tact, temper of mind, or conciliatory manner,' but would be described in much stronger terms, of which the least offensive would be double-dealing. Perhaps the 'modesty' was an out-

[1] Vol. i., p. 166.

come of the 'shyness,' and the not wishing to 'commit himself before strangers.'

It is true he had committed himself to the Tractarians in his practices at least, but not openly. Mr. Purcell tells us: 'Protestant prejudice, popular ignorance, and the hostility of the authorities of their own Church, compelled the unhappy High Church Anglicans to cast a veil of mystery or of secrecy over the practices of confession. Instead of being an ordinary and commonplace act of duty, practised *coram ecclesia*, confession among the Anglicans was, if I may so speak, a hole-and-corner affair, spoken of with bated breath, and carried on under lock and key.'[1]

[1] Vol. i., p. 489.

CHAPTER II.

'AS early as 1839 Manning, enlightened by the teaching of Newman and Pusey as to the spiritual graces of the sacrament of penance, had assumed, as yet in an informal manner, the office of spiritual director of souls. . . . But when new to the office, he felt so disturbed at the insistence of a lady under his spiritual direction to become a Catholic, that in his perplexity he applied to Newman for help and counsel.'[1]

As 'help and counsel,' Newman answered in the following terms:

'Oriel College,
'*Sept.* 1, 1839.

'. . . I think that whenever the time comes that secession to Rome takes place, for which we must not be unprepared, we must boldly say to the Protestant section of our Church: " You are the cause of this; you must concede; you must conciliate; you must meet the age; you must make the Church more efficient, more

[1] Vol. i., p. 232.

suitable to the needs of the heart, more equal to the external. Give us more services, more vestments and decorations in worship; give us monasteries; give us the signs of an Apostle; the pledges that the Spouse of Christ is among us." Till then you will have continual secessions to Rome.'[1]

Newman was already at the date of his letter in the transition stage. Are the 'signs of an Apostle' deceit?

But the voice is not the voice of Newman. It is only the reiterated cry of the children of Israel to Aaron to 'make them gods to go before them.'

Newman wrote to Keble in October, 1840:

'For a year past a feeling has been growing on me that I ought to give up St. Mary's. . . . I am conscious that by means of my position at St. Mary's I do exert a considerable influence on the University, whether on undergraduates or graduates. . . . But this is not all. I fear that I must allow that, whether I will or no, I am disposing them towards Rome. First, because Rome is the only representative of the Primitive Church besides ourselves; in proportion as they are loosened from the one, they will go to the other. Next, because many doctrines which I have held have far greater, or their only, scope in the Roman system.'[2]

We have thus seen Manning as a Tractarian in secret at this period, and we shall now show again by

[1] Vol. i., p. 233.
[2] 'Apologia pro Vitâ suâ,' ed. 1890, p. 132.

his letter to his own Archdeacon, Webber, that he wished to pose publicly as an Evangelical. He excuses his delay in writing by: 'I had to reply at length to a long, indirect letter of a poor friend, who is all but perverted to Romanism. My answer was critical, and delay was likely to do much harm. This will, I hope, plead excuse for me.'¹

Perhaps this was the lady referred to above, who gave so much trouble, and about whom Newman was consulted. But Manning did not tell the Archdeacon that he had any penitents, or that he was a 'spiritual director,' and that, as he had set the stone in motion, he found it difficult to stop it. But the letter served its purpose, as it must have convinced the Archdeacon that he was not a 'Romanizer' in disguise, a character which his Bishop attributed to him.

Mr. Purcell gives an interesting character of him: 'It was in the nature of his cautious and forecasting temperament to study betimes the lie of the land through which his pathway led; to avoid pitfalls; to remove slowly, or by degrees, obstacles in his way; and to seek in prudence by tentative steps the goal of his desires or ambitions.'²

He frightened the old Archdeacon of Chichester into resigning, by piling up the agony in the shape of documents and reports to be filled up, and by asserting that numerous forward steps would have to be

¹ Vol. i., p. 168.   ² Vol. i., p. 172.

taken in the diocese under the new Bishop. The Archdeacon was so thoroughly assured of his strong Evangelicalism that he went so far as to recommend Manning as his successor. Manning was appointed Archdeacon on Christmas Eve, 1840. In writing to Newman to announce his promotion, he said, referring to his Bishop, a Low Churchman and anti-Tractarian: 'I trust I may give him full satisfaction.'[1]

He did not intend to, nor did he, give up his secret practices, but Mr. Purcell shall again sketch his character: 'As Archdeacon of Chichester, cultivating friendly relations with Bishops and Church dignitaries, working in common with statesmen or Cabinet Ministers for the promotion of Church interests, or appearing as an acceptable speaker at great ecclesiastical meetings, to be implicated in any way with the Tractarian party at Oxford would, as he well knew, be destructive alike to his present work and future influence, and fatal to any hope or chance of ecclesiastical preferment. After carefully considering the state of things in regard to his own position and responsibilities, Manning elected to take his stand by the protesting Bishops and to break with Newman and the Tractarian party.'[2]

An Archdeacon's work lies strictly within the diocese in which he holds his archdeaconry, and his duties should not bring him into contact with states-

[1] Vol. i., p. 235.   [2] Vol. i., p. 203.

men or Cabinet Ministers. The Bishops from their place in the House of Lords are fully competent to deal with any question with which statesmen or Cabinet Ministers are concerned. Ecclesiastical meetings are far too frequent for all classes of clergy.

Had the Archdeacons confined their attention to their own duties, the Church would not probably be in the state in which it is at present. Would it be impossible for them, like the school inspectors, to inaugurate 'surprise visits' to churches? They would have their eyes opened in many respects.

The real reason that Manning at this time publicly assisted the Tractarians is given by Mr. Purcell: 'To him the condemnation of Tract XC. was the beginning of the end. Tractarianism was a losing cause. To a losing cause Manning was never partial, early or late in life.'[1]

Manning's first Charge as Archdeacon was delivered at Chichester in July, 1841, and was a strong bid for Low Church popularity and a striking condemnation of the Roman Catholic Church and all its adherents.

Here is an extract from that Charge: 'All foreign Churches, shielded, as they have been, from the storms which have broken upon their despised sister in England, and successful in their unrelenting strife against hearts that yearned for purities, which they had not to give them, have declined and wasted.

[1] Vol. i., p. 240.

The countries most successful against the Reformation, for instance, Spain and France, are the most destitute of Christianity."¹

And in another passage in the same Charge, Manning speaks of the Western Churches as 'inducing to sensual infidelity, and destitute of Christianity.'² It will be well to bear in mind these extracts from the Charge when considering Manning's future utterances.

In his Charge in 1842 he disclaimed all connection with any party in the Church, and in that particular he was not unlike many clergy in the present day, who object to be 'labelled,' and wish to sit on the wall. But in 1843 we find him 'gibbeted by the *Record* as a Tractarian.'³ Perhaps they had got wind of the secret practices at Lavington.

The year 1843, too, was one of considerable excitement, caused by Newman's retirement to Littlemore; and shortly after this latter event, to clear himself from all suspicion, Manning preached his famous 5th of November sermon at St. Mary's, Oxford.

In his Diary, dated November 5, 1845, he states:

'As Fellow of Merton, I had to preach before the University on November 5 (1843)—

'(1) Because such plainness is necessary.

'(2) Because others, who ought, cannot or will not.

'(3) Because my silence is misinterpreted.

¹ Vol. i., p. 207.   ² Vol. i., p. 209.   ³ Vol. i., p. 216.

'(4) Because unsettlement is spreading.
'(5) Because I did not choose either the occasion or subject.
'(6) Because there could be no personality.
'(7) Because it seemed a call of God's providence.'[1]

Mr. Purcell tears these flimsy excuses to pieces in the following note: 'In the above entry Archdeacon Manning states that he preached the 5th of November sermon at St. Mary's as Fellow of Merton, implying that, as Fellow, it was his turn, or duty, to preach on that day. He was not Fellow then; for his Fellowship had ended with his marriage ten years before. Moreover, the Vice-Chancellor, by right of his office, appointed whom he pleased to preach the 5th of November sermon. In 1843 the Vice-Chancellor was Dr. Wynter, of St. John's, a very keen Protestant, and extremely hostile to the Tractarian party.'[2]

Manning had previously, in his Charge in July, 1843, strongly attacked the Tractarians, and it was, no doubt, by some such means as the following, described by Mr. Purcell, that Manning was enabled to pose himself before Dr. Wynter as a staunch Protestant.

Had Dr. Wynter known of the secret practices at Lavington still carried on, he would hardly have ventured to appoint Manning special preacher on such an occasion, and in such excited times.

'It was Manning's invariable habit early and late in

[1] Vol. i., p. 250.   [2] *Ibid.*, note.

life to distribute among his friends, and to send to men of repute in letters or politics, his sermons and tracts. To those who were more intimate with him, or whom he wished to conciliate, he often sent his proof-sheets.'[1]

It seems most extraordinary that, of all those available, Manning should have been chosen to preach the University sermon on such an occasion. His reason that 'others, who ought, cannot or will not' will not hold water. After such an event as Newman's retirement to Littlemore, there must have been many capable Evangelicals who must have felt that silence was no longer possible. Perhaps, if we had had the Diaries intact, and all letters written to or by Manning at this period, we might have found as much intrigue and canvassing of friends as is recorded for us in Manning's life as a Roman Catholic.

What does Manning's third reason imply? 'Because my silence is misinterpreted.' What could have happened between the delivery of Manning's Charge in July, when he publicly and thoroughly broke off all connection with Newman and his satellites, and this 5th of November sermon? This question might have been answered in the Diaries or letters, but we can now only conjecture.

The seventh reason will frequently appear in the course of Manning's life.

[1] Vol. i., p. 136.

'This sermon was preached on Sunday, at St. Mary's, Oxford, and on Monday, November 6, Manning hurried down to Littlemore, in the vain hope of explaining away, or extenuating, his sudden change of front . . . but was met with the answer, "Not at home."[1] Evidently, he must have previously explained away the Charge delivered in July, or there could be no such 'sudden change of front.'

On Newman's retirement to Littlemore, Manning wrote to Dr. Pusey, dating his letter in the absurd fashion which modern Anglicans perpetuate, and which will be a source of untold trouble to future biographers.

'*22nd Sunday after Trinity*, 1843.

'I feel to have been for four years on the brink of I know not what; all the while persuading myself and others that all was well; and more—that none were so true and steadfast to the English Church; none so safe as guides. I feel as if I had been a deceiver speaking lies (God knows, not in hypocrisy). Day after day I have been pledging myself to clergymen and laymen all about me that all was safe and sure. I have been using his books, defending and endeavouring to spread the system which carried this dreadful secret at its heart. There remains for me nothing but to be plain henceforward on points which

[1] Vol. i., p. 248.

hitherto I have almost resented, or ridiculed the suspicion. I did so because I knew myself to be heartily true to the English Church, both affirmatively in her positive teaching, and negatively in her rejection of the Roman system and its differential points. I can do this no more. I am reduced to the painful, saddening, sickening necessity of saying what I feel about Rome.'[1]

This letter was evidently written for publication, and probably was sent round to all his friends and to those whom he wished to conciliate.

Four years takes us back to the year 1839, when, as before stated, Manning inaugurated the sacrament of penance, and assumed the office of spiritual director of souls. He could not plead ignorance of the probable result of that movement, seeing the trouble he had that very year with the lady penitent, and his subsequent appeal to Newman for advice and assistance, and, above all, Newman's answer of September 1, 1839: 'whenever the time comes that secession to Rome takes place, for which we must not be unprepared.' Manning, therefore, well knew the 'dreadful secret at its heart,' and such a letter could only have been written on the supposition that it was most improbable that Pusey and Newman would at that time compare notes. It was written 'as a

[1] Vol. i., p. 251.

deceiver,' and 'with hypocrisy,' as Manning never intended to, and never did, abate his secret practices as long as he remained in the Church of England.

Mr. Purcell tells us: 'How to keep his penitents back from Rome was indeed a perennial trial to Manning from his first case in 1839 to his last in 1851, when he, the spiritual director of so many troubled souls, himself submitted to Rome.'[1] In an autobiographical note Manning states: 'I had never been one of the company of men working in Oxford. I knew them all. I agreed in most things, not from contact with them, but because at Lavington I read by myself in the same direction. . . . I went on reading and working out the sum by myself, and, on looking back, seem to see a constant advance, without deviations or going back; so that my faith to-day rests upon the work of all the chief years of my life. I can see one principle and a steady advance. This I believe to be the leading of the Holy Ghost. Nothing but this would have preserved my intellect from wandering, and myself from resistance.'[2]

From this note it would be gathered that Manning was a great theologian—a second Newman—working out the problem for himself in his country retreat. Though he may not have been in personal contact, he was in continual communication with the 'men work-

[1] Vol. i., p. 233.   [2] Vol. i., p. 259.

ing in Oxford,' perused all they wrote, and contributed himself to their literature under the direction of Newman. How can this note be reconciled with the letter to Dr. Pusey just quoted? Where is the 'one principle and the steady advance'? A staunch Protestant 1833 to 1836; 1837 to 1839 secretly a Tractarian, publicly an Evangelical; 1840 more openly siding with the Tractarians; 1841 to 1842 'unlabelled,' secretly Tractarian; 1843 publicly a strong Evangelical, abusing the Tractarians, but at the same time maintaining their secret practices. The last two sentences of the note are past criticism. 'From his final repudiation of the Tractarians in his Charge July, 1843, to his illness in 1847, he cast in his lot with the popular and winning side. . . . He entered into London society, dined in the company of great people in Church and State, attended levées and drawing-rooms. . . . What wonder, then, that under such influence the hope of preferment, or what he called "elevation into a sphere of higher usefulness," should have entered for a time into the heart of the Archdeacon of Chichester?'[1]

Again: 'Archdeacon Manning's rupture with Newman and the Tractarian party was a turning-point in his Anglican career. Dissociated from an unpopular party and a losing cause—as Tractarianism was regarded on Newman's retirement to Littlemore—pros-

[1] Vol. i., p. 241.

pects of a great ecclesiastical and public career were opened up to the Archdeacon of Chichester. The ambitions of his undergraduate days were revived. It was not now a seat in the House of Commons that he aspired to, but a seat as a spiritual peer in the House of Lords. Mr. Gladstone remembers well Bishop Phillpotts of Exeter saying to him about this period : " No power on earth can keep Manning from the Bench." "It was true at the time," said Mr. Gladstone. "The Bishop of Exeter knew well what he was speaking about ; but not later—not after the full effect of Newman's secession was felt, not after the Papal Aggression outcry, for both we and Disraeli had made up our minds not to give the mitre to anyone connected with the *unholy thing*. But," Mr. Gladstone added, "his tact and moderation, and the art which he possessed in a singular degree of conciliating even the most adverse opinions, made all his friends believe at the time that, like his brother-in-law, Bishop Wilberforce, Manning, in his turn, was sure to receive the mitre." [1]

Manning had now thrown to the winds all pretence of 'love of God and of souls'; but he would no doubt have told us that a 'call' had been received, had he been successful in his ambitious schemes. He is now giving an instance of what, in the autobiographical note written on the occasion of his resignation of his clerk-

[1] Vol. i., p. 261.

ship, he called the 'secularity of the Established Church, from which he had an intense recoil.' Mr. Gladstone evidently knew of his connection with the 'unholy thing,' and did not put much faith in his recantations as published in his Sermons, Tracts, and Charges.

'His private diary of this date bears ample witness to the hopes and ambitions which troubled his spirit and perplexed his judgment, and not infrequently records the remorse of heart he felt at the "secularity" of his life in London. But these confessions and self-examinations must be taken as the shrinkings of a sensitive conscience, wounded by the temptations to a worldly career which for a while beset his heart or imagination. In Manning the instincts of an ecclesiastical statesman predominated over the sensitive spirit and the reforming zeal of a theologian, or the logical conclusions of a thinker.'[1]

What a 'spiritual director of souls'! Of course, he himself confessed and received absolution, but it was not on the principle of 'Go, and sin no more.' He was partaking of the benefit of 'Indulgences.'

What must be thought of the 'sensitive conscience'?

In an autobiographical note Manning says: 'In 1840 I became Archdeacon of Chichester. This at

[1] Vol. i., p. 262.

once brought me into the world in Sussex and in London. I preached often in London, and took part in the chief public meetings. I then went to levées, to drawing-rooms, and dined out, and went to the House of Commons.'[1]

Why should an Archdeacon of Chichester be brought into the world in London? There are in all ninety Archdeacons in the different dioceses of the Church of England. Do they all by their appointments become members of the London world? The truth was that at this time Manning was an ecclesiastical 'guinea-pig.' But a way was seen of remedying this state of affairs by obtaining for him a London appointment, and the ecclesiastical statesman was to blossom forth as a still greater pluralist. The preachership at Lincoln's Inn Chapel fell vacant, and his friends, among whom Mr. Gladstone was most prominent, entered into a strong canvass for his appointment.

In the Diary, November, 1843, we read: 'Gladstone has just put me forward for the preachership of Lincoln's Inn. I have canvassed nobody, and, God helping me, never will, nor even ask anything. I should not have consented even thus far but that I felt I ought to give myself to them that had a right to ask it of me.'[2]

There are more ways of canvassing than by person.

[1] Vol. i., p. 283, note. [2] Vol. i., p. 266.

A friend at Court can wield far more influence than can any candidate by his personal exertions. And we shall find that throughout his life Manning never personally canvassed or asked for anything, but worked the oracle through his friends. He still wished to pose to Mr. Gladstone as one wishing for a 'call,' as the following letter from Mr. Gladstone, dated November 16, 1843, sufficiently shows:

'As to the question of a call to this office, you have every indication of it which can be gathered from special fitness universally allowed, and from highly favourable, though as yet immature, indications on the part of the electors.'[1]

The 'immature indications' were deceptive, and Manning lost the election.

'In 1844 Manning went to Wales to attend the laying of the first stone of a church at Pantassa, dedicated to St. David. The late Lord Denbigh, then Lord Fielding, and his first wife, were friends of the Archdeacon of Chichester, who was their confessor and spiritual director. The church was to be built by Lord and Lady Fielding as a joint thank-offering. In his journal Manning says:

'"*August* 8.—Went . . . to Pantassa for the laying of the first stone of St. David's Church. Met at the schools about sixty clergy; Bishop and Dean of St. Asaph's; long procession—banners, cross, stars,

[1] Vol. i., p. 267.

fleur de lis green and blue, vestments crimson, cross gold—leading up a green lane into a field with broken ground, and a high hill looking down upon it. The clergy went first, with choir chanting the *Te Deum* in Welsh. Lord and Lady Fielding laid the stone, Lord Fielding read the copy of the inscription, and the Bishop said a few words."

'About six years after the laying of the first stone, but before the church was completed or dedicated to Protestant worship, Lord and Lady Fielding became Catholics, and, troubled in conscience about devoting the church which they had built on their own land to the services of the Anglican Church, consulted Archdeacon Manning, as being fully and intimately acquainted with the motives which had induced them to build the church, as well as with all the details of the case. His judgment was that, as owners of the building, they were bound in conscience not to hand it over to the services of a Church in which they no longer believed, and had formally renounced, but to devote it to Catholic uses.'[1]

The 'dreadful secret at its heart' had had its due effect in this case, nor can we be surprised that the two penitents should revolt from the worldly ecclesiastical statesman as confessor and spiritual director.

After the Bishop of the diocese and sixty clergy had

[1] Vol. i., p. 287.

assisted at the laying of the foundation-stone of a church, it is not a little curious to find a dignitary of the same Church, and who had himself been present at the ceremony, advising, when the church is completed, that it should be perverted to other uses. Six years from the laying of the foundation-stone of the church in 1844 would bring us to 1850; but Manning did not publicly profess his faith in the Church of Rome till April, 1851. But we are anticipating. At any rate, we have the man who could write that wonderful letter to Dr. Pusey on the twenty-second Sunday after Trinity, 1843, acting as confessor and spiritual director in August, 1844.

CHAPTER III.

'EARLY in 1845 an attempt was made by the Ultra-Protestant party at Oxford to induce the Heads of Houses to take steps against Newman. Manning, with quick and ready sympathy, sent a letter of condolence. In the hope of appeasing the Ultra-Protestant clamour and of reassuring Bishops and Church dignitaries, excited beyond measure by the results of the Oxford Movement and the dread of Newman's going over to Rome, the Archdeacon of Chichester delivered a Charge in which he exalted once more the Church of England, disparaged by the Tractarians; and once more attacked the Church of Rome, for which Pusey and his followers showed a partial fondness and leaning.'[1]

The following extracts from the Charge delivered in July, 1845, will be instructive:

'Every year deepens in thousands of contrite hearts the tokens of Christ's presence. Every year quickens and unfolds against all antagonistic powers the

[1] Vol. i., p. 305.

spiritual life and fruitful energy of the Church which bore us. And shall any be tempted to mistrust? Shall we ask proofs of our regeneration, or of our waking consciousness, or of the reality of our own soul? There are things which go before all proof— all reasonings rest upon them, logical defences cloud their certainty. Such are our pledges of His presence. They are the tokens of no hands but His; and " if God be for us, who can be against us?" [1]

After anathematizing the Tractarians in the Charge and in the 5th of November sermon, in 1843, and after Newman refusing to see him, what caused Manning to write a letter of condolence to Newman in 1845, and then immediately change front again in this Charge? Why was the Charge sent to Dr. Pusey?

'In acknowledging his Charge of 1845, Dr. Pusey wrote to the Archdeacon of Chichester complaining of the want of love shown to the Roman Church, and especially rebuking Manning for rejoicing over the falling away of Roman Catholics in some of the dioceses of France into schism and heresy, and for encouraging, apparently, the setting up of Protestant teachers. In reply to this rebuke, Archdeacon Manning, August 8, 1845, wrote to Pusey: "We owe to the Church of Rome a pure Christian charity as to a member of the Catholic body; we owe the same also to the Churches of the East. I do not find you

[1] Vol. i., p. 306.

expressing the latter feeling, and that seems to me the cause why you are misunderstood to have not a charity to the whole Body of Christ, but a partial fondness and leaning to the Roman Church . . . Will you forgive if I say it? The tone you have adopted towards the Church of Rome seems to me to breathe, not charity, but want of decision. The Church of Rome for three hundred years has desired our extinction. It is now undermining us. Suppose your own brother believed he was divinely inspired to destroy you : the highest duties would bind you to decisive, firm, and circumspect precaution. Now, a tone of love, such as you speak of, seems to me to bind you also to speak plainly of the broad and glaring evils of the Roman system. Are you prepared to do this? If not, it seems to me that the most powerful warnings of charity forbid you to use a tone which cannot but lay asleep the consciences of many for whom, by writing and publishing, you make yourself responsible."[1]

The staunchest Protestant could not write anything stronger than 'the tone which you have adopted towards the Church of Rome seems to me to breathe, not charity, but want of decision '—and the words are far more applicable to our time than when they were written. We have recently seen an instance of the so-called charity in the action of the Bishops, and a great

[1] Vol. i., p. 308.

majority of the clergy, with reference to the Pope's letter on 'Reunion.' The letter was not addressed to them, but to the people of England, and the latter wisely decided to treat it with the contempt it deserved.

Newman's letter to Spencer on this subject, in January, 1840, would have been applicable:

'The news that you are praying for us is most touching, and raises a variety of indescribable emotions. . . . May their prayers return abundantly into their own bosoms. . . . Your acts are contrary to your words. You invite us to a union of hearts at the same time that you are doing all you can not to restore, not to reform, not to reunite, but to destroy our Church. . . . "The voice is Jacob's voice, but the hands are the hands of Esau."'[1]

Or the same author in the *British Critic* in 1840: .

'By their fruits ye shall know them. We see it (Rome) attempting to gain converts among us by unreal representations of its doctrines, plausible statements, bold assertions, appeals to the weaknesses of human nature, to our fancies, our eccentricities, our fears, our frivolities, our false philosophies. . . . We see its agents smiling and nodding and ducking to attract attention, as gipsies make up to truant boys, holding out tales for the nursery and pretty pictures, and gilt gingerbread, and physic concealed in jam,

[1] 'Apologia pro Vitâ suâ,' ed. 1890, p. 124.

and sugar-plums for good children. . . . We Englishmen like manliness, openness, consistency, truth. Rome will never gain on us till she learns these virtues and uses them ; and then she *may* gain on us —but it will be by ceasing to be what we now mean by Rome, by having a right, not to "have dominion over our faith," but to gain and possess our affections in the bonds of the Gospel. Till she ceases to be what she practically is, a union is impossible between her and England.'[1]

Archbishop Laud felt the same about Rome, as he tells us in his diary :

'*Aug.* 17, 1633, *Saturday.*—I had a serious offer made me again to be a Cardinal. I was then from Court, but so soon as I came thither (which was Wednesday, Aug. 21) I acquainted his Majesty with it. But my answer again was that somewhat dwelt within me which would not suffer that till Rome were other than it is.'

Again, 'The Church of Rome for three hundred years has desired our extinction.' Is it only the Church of Rome that now desires it? How many in the Church of England itself now desire it?

In this same year, 1845, on Samuel Wilberforce being made Bishop of Oxford, and consequently resigning the sub-almonership to the Queen, which he had held under the Archbishop of York, 'the

[1] 'Apologia pro Vitâ suâ,' ed. 1890, p. 126.

appointment, through Wilberforce's interest, was offered to his brother-in-law,'[1] but, 'after a week's anxious deliberation and careful balancing of the pros and cons, Manning resolves to refuse the Archbishop of York's offer,'[2] and in the Diary we have the following:

'I have made up my mind, and will put down my reasons to-night, and, please God, write to-morrow to decline the offer.

> '1. I ought not to be away from my altar at the feasts, especially the Easter Communion— for the sakes (1) of my flock; (2) of my brethren; (3) of my own.
> '2. I am afraid of venturing out of the Church into the Court. . . . If I am to go, then I shall be called again, not less surely for having now refused.
> '3. I owe myself a revenge for Lincoln's Inn, and a greater denial than this.
> '4. I have prayed against pride, vanity, envy, jealousy, rivalry, and ambition, but have done nothing to attain humility.
> '5. I would fain simply deny myself as an offering to Him who pleased not Himself, and perhaps, in a distinction and an honour having worldly estimation, such a denial is better for me than in money and the like.

[1] Vol. i., p. 270. [2] Vol. i., p. 279.

'6. I would fain cross my inclination. Now, in all this Satan tells me I am doing it to be thought mortified and holy; or out of pride, as wishing to slight what others value and assume I should gladly accept.'[1]

These reasons, had they been the expression of the real sentiments of Archdeacon Manning, would have led us to form a very high opinion of his character, but what must we think when we find the following?—

'And yet, on returning to his friends in London, he was once more, as he calls it, "caught up in the whirl of the actual," and accounted himself a fool for having lost a great opportunity in declining the sub-almonership, not for its own sake, but for what it might lead to (as stated in his Diary under date "Feast of St. Paul ").'[2]

We will first give Mr. Purcell's comment on this:

'The self-revelations contained in his Diary bear witness, in the most striking manner, to the supernatural side of Manning's character. His vivid faith, his trust in God, obedience to the Divine will, are made manifest in the struggles which he endured, the temptations which he suffered, and in the victory which he obtained over self. Much as he may have loved "the thrones of the world and the Church," it

[1] Vol. i., p. 279. [2] Vol. i., p. 280.

is clear that his deliberate will and desire was "to be stayed on God."[1]

We will now have Manning's own words (Diary):

'I came home from London last night, after three weeks very ill spent. My life there was irregular, indiscreet, and self-indulgent' (two lines are here expunged). 'Somehow I had thought, before I went to London, that the prospects of elevation would have drawn me under their power. But I come home more estranged from the thought of being raised to any higher place than I went. This is the first year I have found this to be so. Usually I have been powerfully drawn into the whirl of the actual.'—Lavington, July 5, 1846.[2]

Again, in an autobiographical note, written in 1882:

'This appointment was, I believe, the first revival of any thought of an ecclesiastical future which was talked of, and written about, and bragged about me perpetually; and my known intimacy with all the younger men of my own standing, then entered into public life, made people prophesy and take for granted that I was thinking what they thought, and aiming at what they looked for. So far as I know, and can recall, I never put myself in the way of it. . . . I used to be sent for to public meetings and to preach in London. But, as far as I can recall, I never did an act to seek for ecclesiastical advancement."[3]

[1] Vol. i., p. 282.   [2] Vol. i., p. 283.   [3] Vol. i., p. 283, note.

We do not think many will agree exactly with Mr. Purcell's comment given above. Which gives an instance of the 'supernatural side of Manning's character'—the writing good resolutions in a diary overnight, or the virtual tearing them up again as soon as he gets into 'the whirl of the actual'?

Surely, in the autobiographical note his memory must have played him false. And yet he had all the details that we now have, in addition to the now mutilated portions of the Diary and such letters as were not then destroyed, in order to refresh that memory. What meant the 'three weeks very ill spent' in London? What meant the attendance at levées, dinners, and clubs? What meant the 'distribution, among friends and to men of repute in letters or politics, of his sermons or tracts'?[1] Or, again, 'To those who were more intimate with him, or whom he wished to attract or conciliate, he often sent his proof-sheets'?[2] Attention has already been drawn to these practices. Why did he preach the famous 5th of November sermon? And, above all, why did he so constantly change his outwardly-expressed views, and always turn up on what he considered the winning side?

On this question of the refusal of the sub-almonership we get some light from a letter written three years later to Robert Wilberforce:

[1] Vol i., p. 136.   [2] Vol. i., p. 136.

(*Under the Seal.*)

'Rome,
'2nd Sunday after Christmas, 1848.

'... Do you remember asking me at the time of the sub-Almoner affair whether I refused it from unwillingness to involve myself further in our system? I said No, because that was not my fear. I did fear, and put it down at the time, lest the sphere of attraction should bind me in weighing the great doubts which had then fully opened themselves to me.'[1]

Here we have an entirely new reason given for the refusal. And as Mr. Purcell tells us: 'In his letters to Robert Wilberforce, which exceed one hundred in number, Manning is in many ways seen to greater advantage than in anything else which he has written. They exhibit, in the first place, real affection and tenderness. Sincerity and perfect candour mark the whole course and contents of this correspondence. There is no affectation, no reserve, no unreality about it. ... As a seeker after truth, he showed intense earnestness, a deep sense of responsibility, and fear of the Lord.'[2]

Then, the letter last quoted must give the real reason for the refusal of the sub-almonership.

Newman joined the Church of Rome in 1845, and on this occasion, as Mr. Purcell tells us, 'Manning

[1] Vol. i., p. 507.   [2] Vol. i., p. 502.

had a double duty to perform—the duty of private friendship and the duty of public faith and policy. Each duty was performed with consummate tact and skill.'

'London,
'*October* 14, 1845.

'My dear Newman,

'I have only this evening received your letter dated the 8th. If I knew what words would express my heartfelt love of you, and keep my own conscience pure, I would use them. Believe me, I accept the letter you wrote me at such a moment as a pledge of your affection. I shall keep it among many memorials of past days and lasting sorrows. Only believe always that I love you. If we may never meet again in life at the same altar, may our intercessions for each other, day by day, meet in the court of heaven. And, if it be possible for such as I am, may we all, who are parted now, be there at last united! It is a time that admits but few words, and I will say no more than that I am

'Most affectionately yours.'[1]

This letter contrasts curiously with that 'Under Seal,' but we need not look so far ahead, as the following letters show, both addressed to Robert Wilberforce, the first dated Lavington, November 3, 1845:

'What shall I say of our dear friend Newman? My

[1] Vol. i., p. 309.

heart is heavy. I still seem to see great difficulties before us, and wish I could read and talk with you, for we shall have to give plain answers and firm to many hard questions. Not the least part of the difficulty will be to show why principles are safe so far, and no farther.'[1]

And the second, dated December 30, 1845:

'I feel for myself that nothing but a deep and solid foundation such as the Catholic Church has laid (as in St. Thomas Aquinas, Melchior Camus, etc.) can keep a man from intellectual uncertainty and fluctuation. So it is with me. I have never found rest for my foot till I began to see the foundations of systematic theology; and I feel appalled at the thought how little I know, *i.e.*, in its principles.'

The Diary further enlightens us:

'*May*, 1846.—I am conscious to myself of an extensively changed feeling towards the Church of Rome. It seems to me nearer to the truth, and the Church of England in greater peril. Our divisions seem to me to be fatal as a token and as a disease. . . . I am conscious of being less and less able to preach dogmatically. If I do so, I go beyond our formularies. Though not, therefore, Roman, I cease to be Anglican. . . . There seems about the Church of England a want of antiquity, system, fulness, intelligibleness, order, strength, unity; we have dogmas on paper; a ritual

[1] Vol. i., p. 310.

almost universally abandoned; no discipline; a divided episcopate, priesthood, and laity. I seem to feel something by an impression of consciousness not to be reasoned out.

> '1. If John the Baptist were sanctified from the womb, how much more the Blessed Virgin!
> '2. If Enoch and Elijah were exempted from death, why not the Blessed Virgin from sin?
> '3. It is a strange way of loving the Son to slight the Mother.'[1]

If these were Archdeacon Manning's ideas, we cannot be surprised that he was unable to preach dogmatically according to our formularies. But again, to quote the Diary, July 5, 1846:

> '16. I do not feel I should doubt a moment if the choice lay between Rome and any Protestant body.
> '17. It is only because the Church of England seems to me to be distinct from all Protestant bodies that I have any doubt.
> '18. If the Church of England were away, there is nothing in Rome that would repel me with sufficient repulsion to keep me separate, and there is nothing in Protestantism that would attract me.'[2]

[1] Vol. i., p. 484. [2] Vol. i., p. 486.

Mr. Purcell's comment on this is:

'It is curious to note from these entries that the breakdown of Manning's belief in the English Church took place so early as 1846. . . . The evidence to the contrary exhibited in his exhortations to his penitents, which I have recited, I do not think counts for much. They were touching, beautiful little sermons. . . . Such exhortations were formal utterances which he considered it his duty, as their spiritual director, to address to his penitents. His office in the Church, his duty to penitents, the promptings deep down in his soul, laid upon Archdeacon Manning's heart a complicated burden. But to respond to the conflicting claims of conscience by laying down contradictory propositions, though undertaken in good faith, was an attempt in the moral order as impossible as that of squaring the circle. So vain and futile an attempt led, almost of necessity, in various ways to unfortunate misapprehensions and troubles. Imputations cast at the time on his honour and honesty, as he confessed in a letter to Robert Wilberforce, vexed and wounded his heart to the quick. At worst, the double voice which we have seen spoke at times in Manning was the result of a false system, false in many ways in which, unhappily, he found himself involved. What retained Manning so long in the English Church after he had abandoned faith in its mission and teaching, and what entangled his tongue, were not intellectual, but moral difficulties—moral difficulties, which he describes in his Diary as "temptations to secularity"; "shrinkings of flesh and blood," as he tells Robert Wilberforce, from a sacrifice of what was dearest to him in life—his home and hopes; his office and work in the Church of England."[1]

Whatever we may think of this explanation, it is double-dealing in the worst sense; but another letter written to Robert Wilberforce, from whom he had no secrets, and whom he addressed in 'perfect candour and sincerity,' and often 'Under Seal,' shows the matter in a still new light.

(Under Seal.)

'TO MY CONFESSOR IN THE CHURCH OF ENGLAND.

'*June* 16, 1847.

'. . . For the last eight years I have been labouring to keep people from the Roman Church. In 1839 one person, who was all but gone, was settled, and has stood to this day. From 1842 to 1846 Mrs. Lockhart was held back; Miss Lockhart till now. In the beginning of 1846 a man, who had seceded and received Roman baptism, was received back again in Lavington Church. . . . Now let me add a word on a subject I noticed in the beginning—I mean, your fear of my going to Italy. "He that trusteth his own heart is a fool," but I may say that I have passed

[1] Vol. i., p. 487.

through all this before, having been much abroad and already six months in Italy, three in Rome. The effect of this has always been highly repulsive.'[1]

Was this confession false? or was the Diary written a year before false? How can 'If the Church of England were away, there is nothing in Rome that would repel me with sufficient repulsion to keep me separate,' in the Diary, under date July 5, 1846, be reconciled with 'the effect of this has *always* been highly repulsive,' in the confession 'Under Seal' of June 16, 1847? Still more, how can this confession be reconciled with the earlier entry in the Diary, viz., May, 1846, already quoted: 'I am conscious to myself of an extensively changed feeling towards the Church of Rome. It seems to me nearer to the truth, and the Church of England in greater peril'? But, as we go on, we get deeper into the mire. In a letter dated 'Lavington, August, 1846,' he tells Mr. Gladstone: 'I have a fear, amounting to a belief, that the Church of England must split asunder.'[2] Such a confession came as a surprise to Mr. Gladstone.

From that day forth, in all his voluminous correspondence with Mr. Gladstone, Manning never again confessed—at least, until the Gorham Judgment (four years later)—the doubts and difficulties which now began to beset his heart, or his misgivings as to the

[1] Vol. i., p. 467.   [2] Vol. i., p. 316.

future of the English Church; on the contrary, he stoutly maintained in his letters to Mr. Gladstone, as he did in his Charges, Tracts, and Sermons, his unshaken belief in the Church of England. It was to Robert Wilberforce that Manning now transferred the interchange of intimate confidences touching the breaking down of his belief in Anglicanism. And yet to Robert Wilberforce, though he was his 'Confessor in the Church of England,' he could not, as we have just seen, act in a straightforward manner.

Mr. Purcell gives us a short character sketch:

'In such a life as Manning's the action of Divine grace must needs be taken into special account. His nature was peculiarly susceptible to impressions or suggestions, either of good or evil. For instance, his surroundings in London, the sight or society of men of his own standing and acquaintance making their way in life—like Mr. Gladstone in the State, like his brother-in-law, Bishop Wilberforce, in the Church—excited in Archdeacon Manning's breast, as he put on record at the time, feelings of ambition, rivalry, envy; those spurs of the flesh which others might account natural or venial he denounces in the secret chambers of his heart as temptations to sin, to vanity, and worldliness of life. His conscience was sensitive and scrupulous, as the long inward struggle which preceded his refusal of the office of sub-Almoner amply testifies. Deep-rooted in his soul was the fear of God, and the sense of moral responsibility acted as a sharp curb on his action and conduct. The natural man indeed hungered after honour and preferment. The hope of future elevation in the Church was a stay on which his heart rested. In a passage of his Diary I have already quoted, speaking of what he is resting upon, Manning says: "I think it is partly the esteem of others. . . . and on the expectation of something to come."[1]

We are afraid we can only regard his conscience as sensitive and scrupulous as a friend's kindly suggestion. His principles can only be described as 'hand to mouth.' And in such a case conscience plays a very small part. The 'whirl of the actual' and the giving way to (not the tendency to) secularity have, so far in his character, held the predominance. How can we otherwise account for such an entry in the Diary as this, which Mr. Purcell tells us has 'almost a pathetic touch about it'?

'Yesterday morning I had a letter from Burns for a fifth edition of my first volume. This will carry me through 1846, please God; and now I feel at rest. It was great want of faith to be so disturbed. I feel to be in His hands, and He will provide for me, as in this, so in everything.'[2]

Can anything be in worse taste than the latter part

[1] Vol. i., p. 328.   [2] Vol. i., p. 282.

of this entry? Manning had his living, his archdeaconry, and his allowance from his mother. He had no family to support. And yet, after a 'whirl of the actual' in London, he could put down such a sentence as this.

CHAPTER IV.

IN the Diary under the date August 4, 1846, we find:

'The Church of England, after three hundred years, has failed—

' 1. In the unity of doctrine.

' 2. In the enforcement of discipline.

' 3. In the training of the higher life.'[1]

And under date August 6, 1846 :

' I have to-day seen Mrs. Lockhart for the first time since she joined the Roman Church . . . her reckless, cruel, assaulting way of speaking and acting.'[2]

This latter Mr. Purcell explains for us :

' Had she perhaps again aroused his ire by expressing a doubt of the validity of Anglican Orders, as she had done a short time before whilst still an Anglican? On the occasion of the Archdeacon's last visit to her at Chichester, Mrs. Lockhart had ventured to say, ' But, Mr. Archdeacon, are you quite sure of the

[1] Vol. i., p. 449. [2] Vol. i., p. 448.

validity of Anglican Orders?" His answer was astonishingly curt and decided: "Am I sure of the existence of a God?" adding, "You are a good deal too like your dear son." Of this dear son, when he was received into the Church, Manning had said to Mrs. Lockhart, "I would rather follow a friend to the grave than hear he had taken such a step."[1]

This latter sentence sounds startling, but it is only the outward expression, one of the pretty little sermons to penitents.

In the Diary for August, 1846, is the following:

'The Church of England seems to me to be diseased

1. *Organically.*
(1) Separation from the Church *toto orbe diffusa* and from *Cathedra Petri*.
(2) Subjection to civil power without appeal.
(3) Abolition of penance.
(4) Extinction of daily sacrifice.
(5) Loss of minor Orders.
(6) Mutilated ritual.

2. *Functionally.*
(1) Loss of daily service.
(2) Loss of discipline.
(3) Loss of unity: (*a*) devotion, (*b*) ritual.
(4) No education for priesthood.
(5) Unsacerdotal life: (*a*) bishops, (*b*) priests.
(6) Church effaced from popular conscience.
(7) Popular unbelief of mysteries. Insensibility of invisible world.'[2]

---

[1] Vol. i., p. 448. [2] Vol. i., p. 483.

It is astounding to find the separation from '*Cathedra Petri*' put down at this date as an organic disease of the Church of England. How does this agree with the 'highly repulsive' in the letter of June 16, 1847, to his Confessor in the Church of England?

Or, again, how can we reconcile it with, 'I believe one Holy Catholic Church, and I hold the faith of that one Church, believing all it believes, anathematizing all it anathematizes. I believe the Church in England, commonly called of England, to be a member of that one Church; as such I hold to it. If I did not so believe it, I should at once submit myself to the Holy Roman Church.—Fifth Sunday after Trinity, 1849.'[1]

How many more changes are we to see? As to the Diary, we are told:

'*Diary*, 1844 *to* 1847.—Every record, statement, or reflection which he did not think fit for the public eye—nearly half the book—was, late in life, carefully expurgated by Cardinal Manning's own hand.'[2]

Manning was attacked by illness early in 1847, and, to quote the Diary again:

'*February* 23, 1847.—Now, I desire to know how to use this sickness. I desire it may do many things; but one will be enough. If I may, in the spirit of St. Francis' prayer, die to the world: "ut amore amoris Tui mundo moriar." But how can I make this a reality

[1] Vol. i., p. 464.   [2] Vol. i., p. 467.

in my state of life? This I pray God to show me. How can I die to the world?

'1. My kinship surrounds me with ties of blood;

'My priesthood with a flock;

'My archdeaconry with a multitude of persons and relations.

'I need not break with these, but live in them, not for them or by them.

'2. Should I refuse all beyond them? I think not —*e.g.*, London and afar off.

'3. Should I refuse all visits and invitations? Not all—*e.g.*, when asked as a priest, nor when charity may be served.

'But I think I may give up all such of them as I can—never going by choice, or for my own pleasure.

'4. Shall I give up my carriage and servant? I have resolved so to do—at least, for a time —March 23.

'5. Can I make any rules about reading books and topics of conversation?

'6. Is it not rather by longer prayer, and living more to, with, and in God?

'This seems to me (1) what I most lack; (2) what is most direct and dynamical.'[1]

What is the meaning of the date inserted in No. 4? Were the carriage and servant given up from

[1] Vol. i., p. 332.

February 23 to March 23? If this were the case, the Lenten fast would be imposed on the servant.

In the Diary for Lady Day, March 25, 1847:

'*Chief Agents in my Conversion.*
'1. 2. 3. [Lines erased by Cardinal Manning, 1886.]
'4. My admission to Lavington, 1833.
'5. [Entry erased (year of his wife's death), 1837.]
'6. The hearing of confessions, 1844.
'7. The growing up of hope, 1845.
'8. My illness, 1847.

'... I take this illness as a discharge from all subjects of controversy. It is impossible for me to make up my mind on such a matter in my present state, as it may be in the time left to me. At this moment my sole fear of death is my own sinfulness. If He should be pleased to take me, perhaps for ever, it might be safest after my quasi-baptism.'[1]

We should like to have seen the entry in No. 5. Could his penitents have seen No. 6, they would have been considerably astonished to find that the hearing of their confessions by their spiritual director was a 'chief agent' in that spiritual director's conversion.

What hope was growing up in 1845? Was the offer of the sub-almonership a foretaste of future offers to come? He wrote at the time, as we have already quoted: 'If I am to go, then I shall be called again, not less surely for having now refused;' but

[1] Vol. i., p. 334.

then we have the explanatory letter 'Under Seal' to Robert Wilberforce, dated 2nd Sunday after Christmas, 1848, which has also been already quoted. What does he mean by 'quasi-baptism'? Could any honest man have administered what he considered quasi-baptism, as he must have done during the next four years, till he himself joined the Church of Rome, in April, 1851?

'On his two doctors ordering him to go abroad, Manning made the following entry in his Diary:

'"I am willing to lay aside the work I am printing. I am willing to follow step by step, not knowing whither I go. I am willing in my superior will to go where God wills, and for as long and for such an end as He ordains, whether for life or death, that, living or dying, I may be united to Him."'[1]

Again, in the Diary:

'*Voluntas Dei, July* 5, 1847, *Lavington.*—I have just come down from the altar, having offered once more. . . . I never felt the power of love more, nor so much bound to my flock. It is the strongest bond I have—I believe it to be of the reality of the Catholic Church. And yet it will bear no theological argument except a denial of visible unity altogether—which is self-evidently false. To-morrow, by the will of God, I go forth—it may be for a year, it may be for ever. I feel to be in His hands. I know not what is good for me.'[2]

[1] Vol. i., p. 339. [2] Vol. i., p. 342.

In what spirit he started on his journey we shall soon see. Visiting the Frères de la Misericorde at Malines, Manning writes:

'He showed us the relics under the altar, and also others in the sacristy. I could not but feel that the effect of such objects is to awaken and keep alive a high standard of personal devotion—a theory, at least, which we have not. Also the whole objective worship gives a reality we have nothing to equal.'[1]

So thought the Israelites, and therefore desired the golden calf. So think the heathen, who must have an object to represent to them the Invisible Spirit. So think the modern Ritualists, who must have an image or picture of the Virgin Mary, or a crucifix, before which they may bow down. It seems a pity that Archdeacon Manning did not extend his travels further East. Had he seen Mohammedans in a mosque, he would have seen a still higher standard of personal devotion, but he would have seen no 'objective worship.' We might, perhaps, then have seen a still further change of opinion.

In connection with this we may quote from the Diary:

'*March* 29, 1848.—Some time ago S. Broechi, speaking of the Curati, said:

'1. They are despotic, having too much power, *e.g.* of imprisonment, and are corrupted by it.

[1] Vol. i., p. 349.

'2. That he believed they were open to the charge of incontinence; that some treated it very lightly.

'3. That the Regulars, especially the Dominicans, are open to the same charge.'[1]

To which last a note is added:

'Pope Pius IX. made many attempts to reform the monastic orders in Italy, but they were always frustrated by the obstinate resistance of the great religious houses, especially the Dominicans. At the time of the suppression of the religious Orders by the Revolutionary Government of Italy, Pius IX. is said to have declared that, though he was bound to condemn the suppression of the monasteries, in his heart he could not but rejoice, as it was a blessing in disguise. On inquiring, in 1887, of Cardinal Manning whether this reported declaration of Pius IX. were true, his Eminence replied that, whether such an expression of opinion had been actually delivered or not, it truly represented the views of the Pope. The Cardinal added that the success of the Revolution in Italy was in no small degree due to the laxity of morals in the clergy, Seculars and Regulars, and to defective education and training in the Schools.'[2]

Here is an extraordinary admission by a Roman Catholic. If such were the priests, what could they expect the people to be? Was this the result of

[1] Vol. i., p. 386.   [2] Vol. i., p. 386, note.

objective worship? And what a splendid picture of unity! The Benedictines and others even defying the Pope! What are we to think now of the 'functional disease of the Church of England,' 'unsacerdotal life,' 'no education for priesthood'? Had a Protestant made such a statement as that the 'success of the Revolution in Italy was in no small degree due to the laxity of morals in the clergy, Seculars and Regulars,' *i.e.*, to the whole body of the clergy, such a statement would be thoroughly scouted, and would be adduced as an instance of Protestant malevolence. The Church of Rome boasts that it is 'always the same,' and we may take its word for it in this respect.

Here, again, is another important admission:

'I asked him [Milanesi, one of the members of the Circolo Romano] why Acatholic countries were in advance, and Catholic in the rear, of civilization. He admitted the fact.'[1]

It is Archdeacon Manning who asks the question. Such a statement has been made times without number, but has always been jeered at by Roman Catholics.

Newman was bolder than the member of the Circolo Romano, and gave the following answer to the question in his 'Lectures on Certain Difficulties felt by Anglicans in submitting to the Catholic Church.'[2]

[1] Vol. i., p. 388.   [2] VIII., p. 200, ed. 1890.

'The question is this: How is it that at this time Catholic countries happen to be behind Protestants in civilization? In answer, I do not determine how far the fact is so, or what explanation there may be of the appearance of it; but, anyhow, the fact is surely no objection to Catholicism, unless Catholicism has professed, or ought to have professed, directly to promote mere civilization. . . . If, then, Spain or Italy be deficient in secular progress, if the national mind in those countries be but partially formed, if it be unable to develop into civil institutions, if it have no moral instinct of deference to a policeman, if the national finances be in disorder, if the people be excitable and open to deception from political pretenders, if it know little or nothing of arts, sciences, and literature—I repeat I do not admit all this, except hypothetically; I think it is an exaggeration—then all I can say is, that it is not wonderful that civil institutions which profess these objects should succeed better than the Church, which does not. Not until the State is blamed for not making saints may it fairly be laid to the fault of the Church that she cannot invent a steam-engine or construct a tariff. It is, in truth, merely because she has often done so much more than she professes—it is really in consequence of her very exuberance of benefit to the world, that the world is disappointed that she does not display that exuberance always.'

Any State could coin saints in the way Rome has done; many statesmen, by their lives, show such an example as Popes and higher dignitaries of the Roman Catholic Church might well follow. Rome may be unable to invent a steam-engine, but she is responsible for a good many 'inventions,' and more especially fiendish instruments of torture. She needs no lessons in constructing a tariff for Masses and indulgences, and knows how to raise the wind by a 'Jubilee.' But Newman forgot that, when he was lecturing, Rome itself was a 'civil institution.' What was the condition of the Papal States? Was life or property safe even in the environs of Rome itself? Was the cause of the 'national mind being but partially formed' that it had been darkened by superstition? Were the people so accustomed to religious pretences that they were 'open to deception from political pretenders'? In what way, then, did they differ from the present inhabitants of the Soudan? Spain has sunk from a first-rate to the level of a third-rate Power; Italy, the seat of the ancient Roman Empire, dissolved into a series of petty States; but since the Pope has lost his temporal power, Italy has again taken her place among the great nations of the world.

'On reaching Rome, Archdeacon Manning met the Right Hon. Sidney Herbert and his wife, recently married. . . . They both placed themselves under Archdeacon Manning's spiritual direction. . . . In company with Mr. and Mrs. Herbert, Manning attended but very occasionally the English Protestant church outside the walls.'[1]

Of this more anon.

The Diary informs us of the continual visits made during Holy Week, 1848, to different Roman Catholic services, of which we extract the following:

'Went to Cap. Sis. The Gospel, Reproaches, Vexilla Regis. Matins at Chapel of St. Peter's. Lamentations of Jeremiah. Afterwards the exposition of relics from the balcony over S. Veronica; the chapel almost dark; ten tall candles. A pyramidal cross with the spear. A cross, with relic of the true Cross. A frame of silver and gold with the Sudarium, which had a dark centre.'[2]

Who was S. Veronica? The Roman Catholic legend is that she was a woman who wiped our Saviour's face as He went towards Calvary, and that His likeness was miraculously impressed on her handkerchief, and this handkerchief is one of the relics that is shown on great occasions, and the marks of the sweat form the dark centre. The whole story is a vulgar error of a former age, which made the 'veron ikon,' or true likeness of Christ into this woman with a wonderful history.

The spear also is another relic. This is supposed to be the spear which pierced our Saviour's side. In one of the four niches round the great altar of St.

[1] Vol. i., p. 362.   [2] Vol. i., p. 391.

Peter's is a statue of St. Longinus, supposed to be the soldier who pierced our Saviour's side, and said to have been converted by the results of the Crucifixion. The soldier's name was unknown, so they called him Longinus, from the Greek word λογχη, meaning 'a spear.'

The three other niches round the great altar are occupied by statues of S. Veronica, already referred to; of St. Andrew, whose head is supposed to be in the relic chest overhead; and of St. Helena (mother of the Emperor Constantine), so famous for the 'Invention of the Cross.'

St. Helena is said to have found three crosses on Mount Calvary, though, of course, there is no more proof that she was ever there than there is that St. Peter was ever in Rome. St. Helena was unable to decide which was the true Cross, but a sick woman was laid on them in turn, and that on which she was healed was declared the true Cross.

The Feast of the Invention of the Cross is kept in some churches belonging to the Church of England.

In the *Church Times* of May 1, 1896, is an announcement of services at

'Holy Cross Church, Cromer Street, King's Cross.
Feast of the Invention of the Cross.
Sunday, May 3; Wednesday, May 6; Friday, May 8; Sunday, May 10.'

St. Paulinus states:

'The Cross being a piece of wood without sense or feeling, yet seemeth to have in it a living and everlasting virtue; and from that time to this it permitteth itself to be parted and divided, to comply with innumerable persons, and yet suffereth no loss or detriment, but remains as entire as if it had never been cut, so that it can be severed, parted, and divided, for those among whom it is to be distributed, and still remains whole and entire for all that come to reverence and adore it.'

St. Helena at the same time discovered the nails of the Cross, but she threw one into the sea to appease a storm. Her son Constantine used another in the bit of his horse's bridle; of another a crown was made for him by his mother's order; and the iron crown of Lombardy was made of another. In Milan Cathedral there is one elevated above the high altar, between five lights burning day and night. There are three in Rome, three in Paris, two at Naples, and several others in different churches in Roman Catholic countries. In all, there are twenty-seven well-known ones. Godescard says, in explanation, that the true nail is at Rome, in the Church of the Holy Cross, but that it has been filed and no longer has a point, that the filings have been enclosed in other nails made like the true one, and by this means they have been multiplied. St. Charles Borromeo had many nails made like that of

Milan, and when they had touched it they were considered true nails. He gave to Philip II. such a one as a relic.

Whilst on the subject of relics, a few additional particulars may be interesting.

The gown of the Virgin Mary was acquired from an old Jewess and presented to Constantinople in the fifth century. The fête-day of the gown is July 2. There are now eight in different churches in Rome alone, there are six in France, and altogether twenty well-known gowns of the Virgin.

There are seven veils of the Virgin Mary in France, Italy, Spain and Russia, each of which is pronounced the true veil.

There are seven vials of the milk of the Virgin Mary in different churches in Italy, and four in France. At Naples it becomes liquid every time the Feast of the Virgin comes round, but at other times it is dried up; while, on the other hand, at Royaumont it thickens on the feast-day, and is liquid at all other times.

Of John the Baptist there are twelve heads in tolerably perfect condition, besides numerous large fragments of the skull, in addition to seven extra jaws of great note in different parts of Christendom.

Lalaune, in his 'Curiosités des Traditions,' tells us that of 70 saints there are 238 entire bodies in different churches and convents, besides 193 separate heads and 155 hands which belong to 54 of them.

Among these, Sainte Julienne has 20 bodies and 26 separate heads; St. George and St. Pancrace have each 30 bodies. St. Peter has 16 bodies; while Peter the Dominican has 2 bodies, but 56 fingers.

The saints of the Church of Rome have as strange a history as the relics. Professor Max Müller has long ago shown that Buddha has been canonized by the Roman Catholic Church under the name of Josaphat, and that his day is November 27.

But perhaps we ought not altogether to be so much surprised at this, as the Roman Catholics owe so much to the Buddhists. They have borrowed from them their monastic system and their different Orders; their system of Purgatory; their confessors, who were licensed by superior Lamas to receive confessions, inflict penances, and give absolutions; their alms, prayers, and sacrifices for the dead; their monks and friars, with their three vows of poverty, obedience, and chastity; their tonsure; their repetition of prayers with rosary; their use of bells and incense; their works of merit and supererogation; their images, pictures, and fabulous legends; their bowings, prostrations, and turning to the East; their worship of relics, and miracles from them; and, lastly, their worship of the Queen of Heaven and Child.

In Chinese temples behind a screen is a picture of the sacred mother sitting in an alcove, with a child in her arms, and tapers burning before her.

It was on account of this unacknowledged borrowing that the Jesuit missionaries in South America found so little change was necessary when introducing the Roman Catholic religion into that continent.

Such is the result of 'objective worship,' of which Archdeacon Manning seemed so enamoured.

To quote again from the Diary:

'*Sunday, May* 14, 1848.—One Sœur Cardelli told me that there was a monastery of Bavarian Franciscan Sisters near her house of saintly life; one was made Abbess of Novara. As Cardinal Mastai passed to the Conclave, in 1846, she told him he was going to take up a great and bloody cross upon his shoulders. She explained that he was to be elected. After this, Pope Pius IX. sent for her to Rome, and she had revelations of attempts on his life. So they believe; and much more as of the appearance of Satan in token of the trials coming on Italy, and of one of the Sisters carrying the child Jesus through their garden.'[1]

Cardinal Mastai was elected. and became Pius IX. He was evidently one of those who believed all this. Did Archdeacon Manning believe it? We are not told what became of the victims, denounced by this wretched sorceress as conspiring against the Pope's life. Rome is *semper eadem*—always the same. The 'objective worship' always leads to the grossest forms of superstition. It will be well to bear in mind this

[1] Vol. i., p. 404.

story when Manning, after receiving promotion from this very Pope, described him as 'supernatural.'

Mr. Purcell's comments on this part of the Life are perfectly justified. He asks why Manning, 'setting such store as he evidently did on the objective character of Catholic worship, showing such sympathy with its dogmatic teaching,'[1] did not at once join the Church of Rome.

We might ask the same question of the advanced Ritualists of to-day. They go farther in ritual in the English Church than Manning ever did, and openly proclaim that in a Roman Catholic country it is 'breaking the unity' not to go to the Roman Catholic Church.

Again : 'What is most curious and worthy of note is Archdeacon Manning's familiarity with priests and monks and nuns so long before his conversion. Newman never saw a Catholic priest before F. Dominic received him into the Church at Littlemore save two : one an Italian priest, who kindly visited him when he lay ill at Palermo in 1833 ; and F. Damien, the priest at Oxford whom Newman, when he was appointed Vicar of St. Mary's, called upon and claimed as a parishioner. Oakeley told me he never saw or spoke with a Catholic priest until he was received into the Church by F. Newsham. In " Historical Notes of the Tractarian Movement," p. 112, Canon Oakeley said : " I myself

[1] Vol. i., p. 411.

was never in a Catholic church in these islands but once, when I made a speedy retreat under a panic of conscience." [1]

Add to this: 'More difficult of interpretation is the strange silence observed in the Diary in regard to two events of singular interest and importance—viz., Archdeacon Manning's meeting with John Henry Newman in Rome, in 1847, and his audience with the Pope.' [2]

We think the explanation of both these matters may be somewhat easy. Manning was at this time in the 'whirl of the actual,' openly bidding for promotion in the English Church. He well knew the effect of the secessions of the past two years. A considerable number of candidates for promotion had thus been withdrawn. He had influential friends, and no doubt thought that they might be stirred up to greater efforts on his behalf, if they thought that he too was coquetting with Rome. But if, in addition to being intimate with Roman Catholics and attending their services, a report had got wind that he had had an audience of the Pope and an interview with Newman, he thoroughly recognised that his chances of promotion in the English Church would have been gone for ever. It would be interesting to know what was the nature of the bargain made with the Pope at that interview. The first steps of his career in the Roman

[1] Vol. i., p. 412.   [2] Vol. i., p. 414.

Catholic Church point without doubt to some such conclusion.

Again : 'In his Anglican days at Lavington, though he defended in private in his letters and Diary the doctrine of the invocation of saints, and especially of the Blessed Virgin, Manning appears to have had scruples, as Archdeacon of Chichester, about invoking her intercession. For it was only after executing the formal deed of resignation of his office and benefice that he said for the first time the Ave Maria.'[1]

His scruples were dictated by a love of the flesh-pots of Egypt. If he had openly proclaimed these doctrines, he would have been pronounced heterodox, and would have been deprived of his office and benefice. Manning may have never publicly said an Ave Maria, but can we be sure that he had not done so in private?

[1] Vol. i., p. 452.

CHAPTER V.

MANNING wrote to Robert Wilberforce from Rome, February 15, 1848:

'. . . God knows I would rather stand in the lowest place within the Truth, than in the highest without it. Nay, outside the Truth, the higher the worse. It is only so much more opposition to Truth, so much more propagation of falsehood.'[1]

What a splendid sentiment! But was he a 'seeker after truth'? Did he know the elementary meaning of the word? But in what sense are we to take this letter? It was written exactly eight months after the letter written before leaving England, and addressed to the same confessor, in which he stated that 'the effect of this [staying in Rome] has always been highly repulsive.'

Was this written to reassure his friends, whatever they might hear of his doings in Rome?

Let us hear Mr. Purcell:

[1] Vol. i., p. 513.

'What I grant is a curious difficulty, almost startling at first, is to find Manning speaking concurrently for years with a double voice. One voice proclaims in public, in Sermons, Charges, and Tracts, and in a tone still more absolute to those who sought his advice in confession, his profound and unwavering belief in the Church of England, as a Divine witness to the Truth, appointed by Christ, and guided by the Holy Spirit. The other voice, as the following confessions and documents under his own handwriting bear ample witness, speaks in almost heart-broken accents of despair at being no longer able in conscience to defend the teaching and position of the Church of England, while acknowledging in his letters to Robert Wilberforce the drawing he felt towards the infallible teaching of the Church of Rome.'[1]

Where is the truth here? Does the truth consist of deceit?

An explanation is given as follows:

'Manning had, to put it broadly, two sets of people to deal with: the one set, those who put their trust in him—the ecclesiastical authorities and his own penitents; the other set, those in whom he put his trust—his intimate friends and confessors. He dealt with each set from different standpoints: from the one he considered it his duty to conceal his religious doubts and difficulties; to the other he laid bare, as

[1] Vol. i., p. 463.

in conscience bound, the secrets of his soul. On this principle the double voice in Archdeacon Manning is easy of explanation. He had a deep sense of responsibility as an accepted teacher in the Church, and a still deeper in regard to those who came to him as penitents for spiritual guidance.

'The Archdeacon of Chichester knew that he was regarded by his Bishop and the clergy, not only in his own archdeaconry, but in the neighbouring archdeaconry of Lewes — where his orthodoxy had been vouched for by Archdeacon Hare—as a faithful son of the Established Church.'[1]

Did he always feel bound in conscience to lay bare the secrets of his soul? We have seen that on one occasion, at least, he did not feel so bound; viz.: in the Diary of May and July, 1846, and the letter to his confessor of June, 1847. In the former the 'Church of Rome is nearer the truth, and the Church of England in great peril.' And in the latter 'the effect of the Church of Rome has always been highly offensive.'

Mr. Purcell has himself elsewhere, as we have already quoted (p. 48), described the double voice as 'the result of a false system, false in many ways, in which he found himself unhappily involved.' We could not describe it in much stronger terms. What sort of spiritual director must this be, who could thus live a double life?

[1] Vol. i., p. 464.

While Manning was in Rome, Dr. Hampden had been appointed Bishop of Hereford. Dr. Hampden's preferment had given rise to very heated discussions, and Manning, to in some way appease the storm, alluded to the matter in the following terms in his Charge delivered in July, 1848 :

'I am deeply persuaded that in the late contest there are on both sides many of whose truth I have as full an assurance as of my own. . . . Taking the case as a whole, we may begin by distinguishing between the question as to the doctrinal opinions of the right reverend person appointed to that see, and the question as to the manner in which his consecration was effected. Into the former question it is no longer our duty to enter; first, because the Church, as such, has never passed judgment on the theology of Dr. Hampden. He has never been cited and judged before any consistory or tribunal of the Church. Whatever his opinions may be, they are, therefore, unascertained by any authoritative ecclesiastical decision. Secondly, the censure of the University of Oxford in 1846 did not pronounce his doctrine to be heretical, or to savour of heresy, or to be scandalous, or to be offensive to pious ears and the like. It did not specify or characterize the nature of its unsoundness according to the definitions of ecclesiastical usage. It declared in terms just and grave indeed as a censure, but wholly informal and imperfect as a judgment, that he had "so treated theological matters that, in this respect, the University had no confidence in him." So that there exists no formal decision of any tribunal at all, ecclesiastical, or even academical, stamping the doctrine of Dr. Hampden with a specific character of heterodoxy. Until, therefore, any member of the Church be judicially pronounced by a proper tribunal to be unsound, he ought to be publicly treated as orthodox. No man is a heretic to us who is not a heretic to the Church, and no man is a heretic to the Church but one who has been condemned *in foro exteriori* for heresy. Again, it is not only possible, but just, to use this equity of individual judgment; because at various, and some of them most solemn, times—as at the moment of consecration—the right reverend person of whom we speak declared his acceptance of the whole doctrine of faith. He was consecrated not on the confession of his theological works, but on the public subscription of the Catholic creeds. Sincere subscription condemning all heresies is all that has ever been required to reinstate any, however compromised by heterodoxy, in the peace of the Church. Of subscription the fact of consecration is our pledge; of sincerity, who dares a doubt? For these reasons it appears we are now released from the necessity of forming opinions as to past theological statements justly censured, we may accept the last public subscription as a fact closing up a retrospect which nothing but new necessity can reopen.'[1]

Such specious reasoning is worthy of the owner of the double voice. Did Manning intend by this statement to show his influential friends and supporters, all of whom had copies of it sent to them, that, if he were preferred, his consecration, like his illness the previous year, would be a 'discharge from all subjects of controversy,' and a 'fact closing up a retrospect which nothing but new necessity could reopen?'

The following letter written to Robert Wilberforce shows what he really thought of the Hampden appointment:

(*Under Seal.*)
'Lavington,
'*Holy Innocents*, 1849.

'The faith of the Holy Trinity and of the Incarnation subdues me into a belief of the indivisible unity and perpetual infallibility of the Body of Christ. Protestantism is not so much a rival system, which I reject, but no system, a chaos, a wreck of fragments without idea, principle, or life. It is to me flesh, blood, unbelief, and the will of man. . . . The Hampden confirmation and the Gorham appeal show me that the Church of England, supposing it to continue *in esse* a member of the visible Church, is in a position in which it is not safe to stay. But I have

[1] Vol. i., p. 478.

always felt that even these would not move me, if I could by any means sincerely, and in the sight of God, justify the relation of the Church of England to the presence of our Lord ruling and teaching upon earth. I am forced to believe that the unity of His Person prescribes the unity of His visible kingdom as one undivided whole, and that numbers are an accident. It was once contained in an upper chamber; it may be again, but it must always be one and indivisible.'[1]

No doubt, Protestantism, or, in other words, the Church of England, was 'flesh, blood, unbelief, and the will of man' to one who revelled in the 'whirl of the actual,' and was without fixed principles of any description whatever.

The prophecy in the last paragraph of the letter *may* be fulfilled, but its fulfilment will be brought about by the double-dealing of such characters as the one we are now considering.

We will leave the question of 'unity' for the present, as that will more properly come under discussion during Manning's life as a Roman Catholic.

The six following letters cannot possibly be explained away.

To a penitent:

'Lavington,
'*May* 6, 1850.

'1. Judging by the evidence of the Primitive Church, there are many, and they very

[1] Vol. i., p. 515.

grave and vital, points on which the Church of England seems more in harmony with Holy Scripture than the Church of Rome.

'2. The political, social, domestic state of foreign countries as compared with England is to me a perplexity and an alarm.

'3. For three hundred years the grace of sanctity and of penitence has visibly dealt and wrought in the Church of England.

'4. The most saintly and penitent for three centuries have lived and died in it, not only without fear, but with great thankfulness for their lot as compared with another which they have looked on with mistrust, and even more.

'5. I must believe that the spiritual discernment of Andrewes, Leighton, Ken, and Wilson was purer and truer than mine.'[1]

To Robert Wilberforce :

'Lavington,
'*May* 27, 1850.

'. . . Surely the Reformation was a Tudor statute, carried by violence and upheld by political power; and now that the State is divorcing the Anglican Church it is dissolving. What principle of unity, of coherence, do we possess? What principle do we

[1] Vol. i., p. 473.

recognise as Divine? The Bible, the Prayer-Book, private judgment, and Parliamentary establishment seem to me to make up the English Church.'[1]

Letter to his sister, Mrs. Austin:

'Lavington,
'*June* 18, 1850.

'... But first let me tell you to believe nothing of me but what comes from me. The world has sent me long ago to Pius IX., but I am still here; and if I may lay my bones under the sod in Lavington churchyard with a soul clear before God, all the world could not move me.... People tell me to trust and love the Church of England. Who has trusted or loved it more? Who loves it more now, when the foundations of trust are shaken? When have I spoken or written a word in any spirit but of love and reverence, or with any intention but to serve it for Christ's sake? I believe in this you will hold me clear. My contest now is with the State and the world, with secular Churchmen, and those who of a Divine would make it a human society, or, at the best, a Protestant communion.'[2]

Letter to a penitent:

'Lavington,
'*July* 11, 1850.

'When I come to look at the Church of England I see a living continuous succession of Christian people

[1] Vol. i., p. 556.   [2] Vol. i., p. 546.

under their pastors, descending from the earliest ages to this day; and although it has had to bear mutilations and breaches in its external order and in its relations to the other Churches, yet it seems to me to possess the Divine life of the Church, and the Divine food of that life—the Word and Sacraments of Christians. So I have been able to feel hitherto. Late events have called this in question, but it seems to me too soon yet to pass sentence upon it.'[1]

Letter to Robert Wilberforce :

'Kippington,
September 19, 1850.

'. . . I do not know how to resist the conviction—

'1. That the Church of England is in schism.

'2. That it has lost its power to preserve its own internal unity of doctrine and discipline.

'3. That it cannot define, judge, or pronounce with the authority of the Universal Church while it is separate, and in collision with the Universal Church.

'4. That the late events have not changed our position, but revealed it, and that they who see it are bound to submit themselves to the Universal Church. The utter weakness of all that is set up against their conclusions turns

[1] Vol. i., p. 481.

into positive argument in behalf of them. . . .
I feel as if my time were drawing near, and
that, like death, it will be, if it must be,
alone; but I shrink with all the love and
fear of my soul. Pray for me.'[1]

Letter to Robert Wilberforce:

'44, Cadogan Place,
'*September* 26, 1850.

'Surely we want faith, and do not trust ourselves enough to the kingdom which is not of this world. I seem to see how we are called to suffer for faith and for the elect's sake. We have spoken for truth and written for truth; we must now act for truth and bear for truth. Nothing but the suffering of the many can save the Church of England from running down the inclined plane of all separate bodies. It is for it that we are testifying, though it will not see or know it. Newman's going has preserved life.'[2]

It would be interesting to know whether the letter of May 6 was written to the same individual as that of July 11. If so, the penitent was being rather rapidly levelled up; if, on the other hand, they were different persons, what a gap between the two! To his own sister he could not be candid. How had he shown his love and trust in the Church? He loved power, and 'loaves and fishes,' and the 'whirl of the actual';

[1] Vol. i., p. 560. [2] *Ibid.*

but what else? How could he write such a sentence as, 'When have I written or spoken a word in any spirit but of love and reverence?' when we have seen what he had written in his letters and diaries, and how he had behaved in Rome? Was he, of all others, the one to wage a contest with 'secular Churchmen'? At all events, his first contest would be with self.

His 'time' has been very long 'drawing near.'

It was in May, 1846, according to his Diary, that he found the 'Church of Rome nearer the truth.' But he did not go yet. Was the bargain that he made with the Pope at his interview in Rome, that he should bring many with him, the cause of the 'shrinking with all the love and fear of his soul' at going alone. Perhaps the divining nun had warned Pius IX. that Manning had not yet a sufficient following and therefore the going was put off.

We shall see in due course to what extent Manning was called upon to suffer for what he called 'truth.'

The Church of England did not then, and does not now, appreciate his testimony. It would have been better for her, for him, and for religion generally, if he had gone seven years before.

But the most extraordinary sentence is, 'Newman's going has preserved life.' How was this? Newman had joined the Church of Rome five years before.

Were the first seeds of the future jealousy already taking root?

Manning writes another letter to Robert Wilberforce, dated:

'Lavington,
'*October* 22, 1850.

'... I am not afraid of seeming to fly from a storm. No one worth thinking of would think so, and multitudes, very well worth thinking of, think me all but dishonest. Public honour is essential to character and usefulness; and I feel sure that my work in the Church of England is over. I hinder more than I help.'[1]

If multitudes, knowing only the outside appearance, thought him all but dishonest, what will multitudes who can now see both faces think of him?

Jabez Balfour thought public honour 'essential to character and usefulness.'

Though Manning acknowledged, 'I hinder more than I help,' the final step was not taken for yet another six months. What was the cause of the delay?

Mr. Purcell's comment is hardly to the point:

' But since there was no way of escape permitted by conscience, nor of delay even, Manning was too upright a man, too God-fearing by far, of a temper too heroic, to flinch from the consequences, be they what they may, of an act dictated by faith.'[2]

[1] Vol. i., p. 564.   [2] Vol. i., p. 595.

Manning wrote, on January 28, 1851, to Laprimandaye, his former curate and one of his confessors, who had just joined the Church of Rome:

'But I may say to you, and to you alone, that I cannot think to be long as I am now. I have been dealing, one by one, with the many bonds of duty which bind me on every side, unravelling some and breaking others. I owe still some acts of deliberation to particular persons. When they are discharged I shall believe that I stand before God all alone, with no responsibility but for my own soul.'[1]

Then, by this last sentence, the 'particular persons' alluded to were his penitents. In October, 1850, the Papal Bull restoring the Catholic hierarchy in England was issued, to which Lord John Russell replied by raising a 'No Popery' cry. The Bishop of Chichester called on Manning, as his Archdeacon, to summon a 'No Popery' meeting. At the meeting Manning announced his intention of resigning all his appointments in the Church of England.

Mr. Purcell tells us:

'Five or six years ago the Cardinal said, "Shall I tell you where I performed my last act of worship in the Church of England? It was in that little chapel off the Buckingham Palace Road. I was kneeling by the side of Mr. Gladstone. Just before the Communion Service commenced, I said to him, "I can no

[1] Vol. i., p. 597.

longer take the Communion in the Church of England." I rose up—"St. Paul is standing by his side"—and, laying my hand on Mr. Gladstone's shoulder, said, "Come." It was the parting of the ways. Mr. Gladstone remained, and I went my way. Mr. Gladstone still remains where I left him.'[1]

Is this the explanation of the long delay? Was it Mr. Gladstone he was waiting for? Was this the 'last bond of duty to be unravelled or broken'? The situation was certainly dramatic, but surely Cardinal Manning meant, 'Saul [before his change of name] is standing by his side.' No one could in any sense compare Manning with St. Paul.

[1] Vol. i., p. 617.

CHAPTER VI.

IN an autobiographical note Manning tells us:

'On April 6, 1851, Passion Sunday, Hope and I went to F. Brownbill, in Hill Street, and were received—I before High Mass, he after it. So ended one life, and I thought life was over. I fully believed I should never do more than become a priest; about which I never doubted, or even wavered. But I looked forward to live and die in a priest's life, out of sight. I went to St. George's and saw the Cardinal; he fixed to give me Confirmation and Communion the following Sunday. He then told me he had decided to ordain me priest without delay, and that he did so with the knowledge and sanction of Rome.'[1]

'Manning's receiving Holy Orders in so short a time as ten weeks after his reception into the Church gave rise to rather severe criticisms on Cardinal Wiseman's precipitancy.'[2]

Part of the bargain with the Pope was being already

[1] Vol. i., p. 627. [2] Vol. i., p. 628, note.

fulfilled, and we shall see further considerable developments.

'To Mr. Allies, announcing his intention, after the Gorham Judgment, of becoming a Catholic, Archdeacon Manning replied: "Samuel waited till God called him three times. This is not your third call." It was, indeed, not Manning's. His first call was the Hampden appointment; the Gorham Judgment the second; and the third call, as he wrote to Lord Campden on January 14, 1851, "this Anti-Roman uproar."'[1]

How can the Hampden appointment be his first call, considering the contents of his Charge delivered July, 1848, of which we have already given extracts? In that Charge he completely whitewashed Dr. Hampden, and administered a rebuke to those who had condemned him.

'At a banquet given in honour of Cardinal Wiseman, at Arundel Castle, by the then Earl of Arundel and Surrey, there was a large company which included many recent converts, among them Manning and Mr. Allies. Cardinal Wiseman, speaking to Mr. Allies and others in allusion to Manning, said, "I hope soon he will be one of us." The confident tone in which Cardinal Wiseman spoke, as well as the substance of the remark, made at the time a deep impression on Mr. Allies, for Manning had only just been made

[1] Vol. i., p. 631.

priest, and had not yet commenced his theological studies and training. And yet Wiseman was already expressing a hope of Manning soon becoming a Bishop.'[1]

The bargain with the Pope was evidently well known to Cardinal Wiseman. What becomes of 'I fully believed I should never do more than become a priest,' in the autobiographical note already quoted?

So ends Manning's life of deceit and hypocrisy in the Church of England, but we have one more extract to make:

'On learning, in January last (1895), the substance of Manning's letters to Robert Wilberforce, Mr. Gladstone was surprised beyond measure. Speaking with evident pain, he said: " To me this is most startling information, for which I am quite unprepared. In all our correspondence and conversations, during an intimacy which extended over many years, Manning never once led me to believe that he had doubts as to the position or Divine authority of the English Church, far less that he had lost faith altogether in Anglicanism. That is to say, up to the Gorham Judgment. The Gorham Judgment, I knew, shook his faith in the Church of England; it was then that Manning expressed to me—and for the first time—his doubts and misgivings. I won't say that Manning was insincere—God forbid!—but he was not simple

---

[1] Vol. i., p. 638.

and straightforward as, for instance, Robert Wilberforce, the most simple and candid of men."'

Manning's Anglican correspondence with Mr. Gladstone was even more copious than with Robert Wilberforce, for it extended over a longer period. Mr. Gladstone said: 'Over a long period every subject of vital interest affecting the Church of England was discussed by Manning with masterly ability and foresight. His letters were a striking record of every movement in the Church of England during a most trying period, especially since Newman's secession.' On learning that Manning's Anglican letters were no longer forthcoming—had, as far as could be ascertained, been destroyed by the Cardinal not long before his death—Mr. Gladstone was greatly pained, and exclaimed: 'Had I dreamt that Manning would have destroyed those letters, I would never have returned them to him. Neither in those letters nor in conversation did Manning ever convey to me an intimation, or even a hint, that he had lost faith in the English Church. On the contrary, I remember, as if it were yesterday, a remarkable conversation I had with him in the summer of 1848, just after his return from Rome. We were walking through St. James's Park . . . referring to his illness of the previous year, Manning said, in the most solemn manner: "Dying men, or men within the shadow of death, have a clearer insight into things unseen of others—a deeper knowledge of all that relates to Divine faith. In such a communion with death and the region beyond death, I had an absolute assurance in heart and soul, solemn beyond expression, that the English Church—I am not speaking of the Establishment—is a living portion of the Church of Christ."'[1]

It must be remembered that the illness, during which he made such numerous good resolutions, preceded the journey to Rome, where he showed such pleasure in attending the Roman Catholic functions, and from whence he wrote to Robert Wilberforce: 'I would rather stand in the lowest place within the Truth, than in the highest without it. Nay, outside the Truth, the higher the worse. It is only so much more opposition to Truth, so much more propagation of falsehood.' As this was written on February 15, 1848, and we know what his real sentiments were long before that period, he is convicted out of his own writings of propagating falsehood for more than three years.

'In the early morning of December 4, 1851, Monsignor Hohenlohe called on Manning, at 28, Via de Tritone, and said it was the Pope's express desire that the neophyte should commence at once his studies at the Accademia Ecclesiastica. This academy, attended chiefly by young ecclesiastics of high rank or of distinguished talents—for it is the

[1] Vol. i., p. 569.

school in which the future diplomatists of the Vatican are trained—is commonly called the "nursery of Cardinals."[1]

Extraordinary attention on the part of the Pope, and utterly inexplicable on any other hypothesis than that we have before given.

Cardinal Manning gives the following explanation in his Journal, 1878 to 1882 :

'. . . These events—my ordination and my residence in Rome—were decided by authority for me, and I only obeyed, and from these all have followed now for twenty-eight years. . . . I remained in Rome from 1851 to 1854, going home during the great heat of summer to England. It was a time of great peace, but of great trial. . . . During those three years I received from Pius IX. a fatherly kindness. I saw him nearly every month, and he spoke with me freely on many things, and gave me freedom to speak to him. It was the beginning of the confidence which was never broken. I owe to Cardinal Wiseman and to Pius IX. all that has befallen me in my Catholic life. I never asked of them, or of anyone in my former life, anything whatsoever. All that has come upon me has come without any seeking.'[2]

The same statement about 'asking' has been made before ; but it was then called 'canvassing,' and is

[1] Vol. ii., p. 10.   [2] Vol. ii., p. 18.

true in a sense, but it depends on what 'seeking' means, whether we can recognise that statement as partially true too. He undoubtedly sought for his Fellowship, his living, his archdeaconry, and he also sought for a bishopric. Had he been promoted to the latter, there is not much doubt he would have remained in the Church of England to the day of his death. It would be at least curious if, with his great intimacy with Mr. Gladstone, he had not been informed, perhaps in an indirect way, that he had no chance of such preferment.

We have an answer ready to our hand as to the early days of the Roman Catholic life.

'In the year 1853 or 1854, when Manning was studying theology in the Accademia Ecclesiastica, Mgr. Talbot, of the Vatican, met in Rome Mr. James Laird Patterson, of Trinity College, Oxford, who, after his travels in the East, had just become a Catholic. Speaking of the most recent converts, one of whom was then studying at the Accademia Ecclesiastica, Mgr. Talbot asked, half in jest, half in earnest, "whether a man who was already manœuvring for a mitre would make any the worse a Bishop for that."'[1]

Of course, 'manœuvring' can neither be called 'asking' nor 'seeking'; but it partakes a little of both.

[1] Vol. ii., p. 17, note.

To turn again to the Diary:

'*Passion Sunday*, *March* 27, 1852. [Here a line or two erased.] This I believe to be Satan's work, and favourite snare for me. I am soft, longing, and regretful. . . . I have had, since Monday night, a strange sense of joy, yet of restraint [here two pages are cut out]. Saturday . . . went down and found the Blessed Sacrament exposed in church. Said rosary with a hard, absent heart; carried a taper to the altar, and felt as if I had seven devils—Judas—and a hypocrite, and, as I went forward, as if I might fall dead.'[1]

'*April* 5, 1852.—Last night I was very much tempted to make an example of someone who busies himself in setting about reports of me. But this morning, meditation before Mass completely changed me.'[2]

'*November* 22, 1852.—Since Friday I have been suffering an intense anguish. A horror falls on me lest I should be falsely accused of a thing, of which God knows my innocence. Till two things came to me:

'1. To offer my lifelong shame in union with the shame of my Lord. So His name be glorified and His elect be gathered.

'2. To conform myself to St. Francis de Sales' example. He was slandered with apparent

[1] Vol. ii., p. 12.   [2] Vol. ii., p. 14.

proof. He was a Bishop in full work; had a house of religious; was believed guilty by all but a few; was three years under a cloud; but would have no defender but God. He waited in silence, and went on as before. God give me grace so to do. To-day I put myself under St. Francis de Sales' patronage in this point.'[1]

We cannot, of course, tell what was the cause of this 'intense anguish,' but as 'lifelong shame' was to be offered, the accusation cannot have been altogether a false one. No man can have a lifelong shame on account of a false accusation.

The offering the 'lifelong shame in union with the shame of my Lord' is flat blasphemy; but we shall get accustomed to that. We have already seen Manning comparing himself to St. Paul. But Pope Pius IX., as we shall presently see, went further still. On an autocratic exercise of his own power against the wish of his Council, the Pope described it as 'a *coup d'état* of the Lord God.'

Cardinal Newman gives us some explanation of this practice in his 'Lectures on Certain Difficulties of Anglicans in submitting to the Catholic Church' (No. IX., p. 232):

'Listen to their conversations; listen to the conversation of any multitude or any private party; what

[1] Vol. ii., p. 15.

strange oaths mingle with it! God's heart, and God's eyes, and God's wounds, and God's blood. You cry out, "How profane!" Doubtless, but you do not see that the special profaneness, above Protestant oaths, lies not in the words, but simply in the speaker, and it is the necessary result of that insight into the invisible world which you have not. Your people would be as varied and fertile in their adjurations and invocations as a Catholic populace, if they believed as we.'

What can we think of such special pleading? We know the Roman Catholics have cut out the second commandment. Have they practically treated the third in the same manner?

St. Alphonso de Liguori, in his 'Moral Theology,' IV. 2, 146, takes entirely different ground :

'We must mark that generally men who angrily utter words such as "By God! by Christ! I will kill you!" commit no grave sin, as they are for the most part excused on the ground of ignorance or want of deliberation.'

Then, the command 'Thou shalt not take the Name of the Lord thy God in vain' is of no effect. We were told so often in Manning's Anglican life that he was 'stayed only on God'; but we find he is now stayed on St. Francis de Sales as well. No other meaning can be put to 'To-day I put myself under St. Francis de Sales' patronage in this point.' Perhaps Newman would say we have not the 'insight into the invisible world.' The modern spiritualists, however, claim this insight in a very high degree. But their methods are at present slightly under a cloud, and we cannot help thinking the 'Life of Cardinal Manning' will have the same effect on the Ritualist and Roman Catholic systems.

Such is the effect of 'objective worship.' The ancient gods of Greece, Rome, and the heathen world generally are turned into more modern 'saints,' and their protection is in the same way invoked.

We subjoin a description of St. Bridget as a proof of this. It is taken originally from the MS. called the 'Leabhar Breac,' in the library of the Royal Irish Academy, and it was included in 'The Patrons of Erin,' written by W. G. Todd, D.D., and printed in 1859 by the Catholic Publishing Company.

'The father of this holy virgin was the Heavenly Father; her son was Jesus Christ; her tutor was the Holy Spirit; and it was therefore that this Holy Virgin performed great and innumerable miracles. It is she that relieves everyone that is in difficulty and danger. It is she that restrains the roaring billows and the anger of the great sea. She is the prophesied woman of Christ. She is the Queen of the South. She is the Mary of the Irish.'

CHAPTER VII.

WE have given the short extracts from the Diary (quoted above) more particularly for the purpose of contrasting them with the letters written to Robert Wilberforce during the same period.

Manning was very anxious for Robert Wilberforce to follow in his footsteps, and, no doubt, still more so that he should have the credit of bringing in such a convert.

The following are extracts from the letters:

'Rome,
'*March* 6, 1852.

'... Unceasingly I felt the consciousness that the Church of England is out of harmony and obedience to the truth and will of our Divine Lord; and all in it that is good and true is of no avail until the act of restitution and submission is made. ... It is no question of detail, but of the first absolute vital principle. Does our Divine Lord now teach in the world by the guidance of His Spirit, and by what organs? All the rest, all particular doctrines, and all piratical corruptions and abuses, even though they were as great as those of Jerusalem at our Lord's coming, are all of no weight in the great controversy between truth and conscience. . . . All I fear for you is chronic doubt, and the dimness which delay spreads over the clearest evidence. I believe that nothing will, because nothing can, go beyond the revelations of the last three years to prove that the Church of England is a human society, out of the sphere and guidance of the Divine Spirit.'[1]

In a letter written from Birmingham on July 11, 1852, he says:

'I have no words to express what is the Divine life and Divine reality of the Church in its acts.'[2]

Again, from London on August 12, 1852:

'. . . Since I could look upon Anglicanism, and especially on the line of our friends such as Pusey and Keble, as a bystander, and with the guidance of real and certain theology, I am alarmed, not so much at the doctrinal errors, as at the false view of moral probation which they inculcate. . . . Surely your very trial is, not to be carried passively away, but to act. And delay brings chronic indecision, and multiplies social and home difficulties, and weakens our power of volition.'[3]

[1] Vol. ii., p. 27.   [2] Vol. ii., p. 29.   [3] Vol. ii., p. 30.

Again, on September 28, 1852, he writes:

'... And now I will try to say what occurs to me about your questions. They appear to me to a great extent needless difficulties foreign to theology.

' 1. The Council of Trent says that our Lord's humanity, " secundum naturalem existendi modum," *i.e.*, in its proper dimensions, etc., is at the right hand of God only.

' 2. The Church therefore distinguishes natural presence from supernatural or sacramental presence.

' 3. The presence, being supernatural, is not a subject of natural criteria or natural operations.

' 4. Within the sphere of natural phenomena and effects there is no change in the consecrated elements; but a change does take place in a sphere into which no natural criteria such as these can penetrate. Of this we are assured by the words of revelation, " Hoc est," etc. The Church is concerned only to affirm this supernatural fact, as Vasquez says, "ut sint vera Christi verba." Beyond this affirmation the Church affirms nothing.

' 5. It has no jurisdiction in science or philosophy. The office of the Church is Divine and unerring within the sphere of the original revelation.'[1]

[1] Vol. ii., p. 31.

Again, on October 26, 1853:

'... You have no foundation but human judgment, and therefore you are "tossed to and fro and carried about" by words of men. To me this is simply impossible, because I believe on the basis of a Divine Teacher.... When you say that the Roman Church is not historically the same, is it not to say, *My* view of its history differs from its own? But may not the Catholic Church know its own history better, and by a lineal knowledge and consciousness to which no individual can oppose himself without unreasonableness? I am perfectly persuaded that the Catholic Church is historically the same in personal identity and functions.'[1]

On January 20, 1854:

'... If the doctrine of the Holy Trinity be true, the Holy Spirit now teaches in the world; and if the Holy Spirit now teaches in the world, the Church of God is infallible. A present and practical Divine teacher is in the world, from whom lies no appeal to the Bible or to antiquity. I do not say what it is. It is enough to say it is not Anglicanism.'[2]

On February 5, 1854:

' Mary writes me word that you are scandalized with St. Alphonsus.... I bind myself to prove ... that Alphonsus teaches as follows:

' 1. That to speak falsely is, under all circumstances

[1] Vol. ii., p. 35.   [2] Vol. ii., p. 36.

and conditions, intrinsically and immutably a sin.

'2. That the examples he gives of execrable ambiguity, he gives on the ground that they are not falsehood.'[1]

On February 28, 1854:

'... You say quite truly, "St. Alphonsus does not say that you may lie, but he says that is truth which is a lie." Therefore, St. Alphonsus (1) condemns falsefood; (2) allows certain expressions, because in his judgment they are true.... They (his principles) seem to me to be as clear as day, as follows:

'1. That to speak falsely is a "malum intrinseci," and always a sin against God. Nothing can justify it. Innocent III. declares that "etiam pro vitâ defendendâ nunquam licet mentiri."

'2. That when interrogated lawfully by those who have a right to interrogate, we are bound to disclose all our knowledge in the matter of the interrogation.

'3. That, when interrogated by those who have no right, or in an unlawful way, we are not bound, but may set aside the questions by any lawful means.

'4. That to lie is not a lawful means — as above, No. 1.

[1] Vol. ii., p. 37.

'5. That to use "restrictio pure mentalis," *i.e.*, when the words heard are false, is falsehood—condemned by Innocent XI.

'6. That to use words which are true but ambiguous is lawful; that is, "restrictio non pure mentalis," because the words are true without any mental supplement.

'All St. Alphonsus' cases come under this head. The only question is whether the instances are admissible, for the principles are not to be denied. . . . Most earnestly do I pray that you may be delivered from the whole system of insincerity by which you are surrounded.'[1]

On Holy Thursday (April 13), 1854:

'. . . When I said St. Alphonsus only is at stake, I mean the Church is clear through Innocent III. and Innocent XI. The most could be that the congregation which examined St. Alphonsus' works failed of their due diligence, and that St. Alphonsus is open to censure. But they were sixteen years upon his works. And having read every word of St. Alphonsus, I am convinced that they said right, "Nihil crusurâ dignum." The question is, Who knows St. Alphonsus' meaning? I *know* that he is misrepresented, and that the propositions I gave are his, and common to all theologians. But enough of this. After three years I do not speak, as you admitted, like a Mormonist or Swedenborgian,

[1] Vol. ii., p. 38.

when I say, one God, one Spirit of Truth, one Church, one theology, one living Judge, authoritative only because Divinely guided. Never for one moment in these three years has my reason or will wavered in this faith founded on profuse conviction of the reason, with the fullest counterproof from experience. Anglicanism is to me human, fragmentary, and a dishonour to our Lord and to the redeemed intelligence.'[1]

On May 19, 1854:

'... I declare on my own knowledge (1) that in miracles, legends, and all the things in his (Merrick's) satirical catalogue, not one presents to my mind, or to the mind of the poorest Catholic, the sense in which he understands them.... (3) That the educated Romans (Italians generally, French still more so) deride the English Church as the lowest form of worldly and inconsistent Protestantism.... The whole is a silly gossip, almost as bad as your talking of your being required to carry out the system of St. Alphonsus. You are an old Yorkshireman, and you know that you, as I, are required to carry out the system of no man.'[2]

And, lastly, July 4, 1854:

'... Does not authority really mean evidence, or the reason why we believe certain truths? Not "sic volo, sic jubeo," etc. ... I have read every word of St. Alphonsus' "Moral Theology," both the lesser and

[1] Vol. ii., p. 40.   [2] Vol. ii., p. 42.

the greater, and the "Treatise on Equivocations on Oaths" again and again. I know that it is misunderstood and misrepresented; that it needs only to be read with sincere attention. But, like everything which is not superficial, if taken up as Merrick has done, it is simply unintelligible. He sought for scandals, and he has made them for himself. I say this because I have abundant proof that he does not understand the elementary principles of moral theology. . . . May not those who revised St. Alphonsus understand him rightly, and you otherwise? It is a fact that St. Alphonsus allows certain equivocations, even firmed with an oath. But he considers them to be truths, and therefore lawful.'[1]

Was it the truth that 'never for one moment in these three years has my reason or will wavered in this faith'? What meaning, then, is to be assigned to the entry in the Diary under date March 27, 1852: 'This I believe to be Satan's work and favourite snare for me. I am soft, longing, and regretful'? Was the double voice still in existence? Had Manning so often deceived others, that at last he had deceived himself?

Robert Wilberforce wavered till after the death of his wife, and did not join the Church of Rome till September, 1854. If he was led to take this step by the specious arguments in these letters, we cannot rate his understanding very high.

[1] Vol. ii., p. 43.

We will now criticise the letters in detail.

Does Cardinal Manning mean, in the letter of March 6, 1852, that 'all particular doctrines and all piratical corruptions and abuses' of Rome, 'even though they were as great as those of Jerusalem at our Lord's coming, are of no weight in the great controversy between truth and conscience' which would force a man to join the Church of Rome? What was the fate of Jerusalem? What would be the fate of Rome if our Lord came now?

Had Cardinal Manning read Matt. ix. 36-38? Our Lord came to a Church whose shepherds traced back their lineage to Moses; a Church gathered together as no flock ever was; a Church that had a most perfect organization and ritual, and yet our Lord described this Church as a flock of helpless sheep scattered over the plain, lying down faint from very weariness because they had no shepherd.

What is the warning to the Church in Sardis? 'I know that thou hast a name that thou livest, and art dead.' And the still more awful warning addressed to the Church in Laodicea? Are these warnings in no way applicable to the Church of Rome? We shall probably see some good cause for thinking that they are, as we proceed in this Life.

We magnify our own faults in others. Surely Manning was the last person in the world to lecture on the effects of chronic doubt, delay, and indecision.

As to the 'Divine life and Divine reality of the Church in its acts,' we shall see the intrigue and treachery on which those acts were founded, and shall be able to appreciate them at their true value. We can understand his objection to what he called the 'doctrinal errors' of the English Church; but did Manning judge of the 'moral probation' by his own deceit and double-facedness when a member of that Church? Was his 'moral probation' any better in the Church of Rome?

With regard to the answers to questions in the letter of September 28, 1852, Manning refers to the Council of Trent; but the doctrine of Transubstantiation had been affirmed three hundred and fifty years earlier by the Lateran Council, in A.D. 1215, and was in no way interfered with by the Council of Trent.

It has been well said that if the words 'Hoc est meum corpus' are to be taken literally, our Lord, on instituting the Last Supper, partook of His own Body and Blood. Why cannot the Roman Catholics say at once that they treat the Body of Christ in the same manner as they do the relics of saints—which they multiply indefinitely, as we have seen?

The priest on his consecration receives the wonderful power of 'making the Body of Christ,' and becomes by that consecration a mediator between God and man —as St. Thomas Aquinas tells us: 'Sacerdos constituitur medius inter Deum et populum' (Summa, iii. 22).

How do they read 1 Tim. ii. 5: 'For there is one God, and one mediator between God and man, the man Christ Jesus'? What place is there here for the intercession of the Virgin Mary?

Why was the Council of Trent referred to when it altered no points of doctrine or morals? Was Robert Wilberforce likely to be influenced by the acts of this Council? We know that modern Anglicans sometimes refer to the Council of Trent as if its decrees should be binding on every Church. But leaving aside the question of the composition of that Council, we much doubt if any Anglicans, after reading the account of Manning's acts in, and his account of, the Infallibility Council of 1870, will have any confidence in the acts of any Council. That the Church 'has no jurisdiction in science or philosophy' is certainly a development which Newman might have enumerated in his famous 'Essay.'

But Newman, on the other hand, after he became a Roman Catholic, stated distinctly: 'The Catholic Church claims, not only to judge infallibly on religious questions, but to animadvert on opinions in secular matters which bear upon religion, on matters of philosophy, of science, of literature, of history, and it demands our submission to her claim' ('Apologia pro Vitâ suâ,' ed. 1890, p. 257). And again: 'I have not to speak of any conflict which ecclesiastical authority has had with science, for this simple reason

—there has been none' ('Apologia pro Vitâ suâ,' ed. 1890, p. 264).

Was it forgotten that Galileo had been forced to recant? Manning had not forgotten it, as in an autobiographical note, dated February, 1887, he says:

'... I look for a reassertion. Their pride will not let them say, after all, that the earth moves.'[1]

In the letter of October 26, 1853, Manning states that the Church of Rome is historically the same in personal identity and functions.

Cardinal Bellarmine says the whole cause of Christianity depends on the Pope's supremacy: 'De quâ re agitur cum de Primatu Pontificis agitur? Brevissime dicam; de summâ rei Christianæ.'

Dom de Vaines, the Benedictine, in his 'Dictionnaire Raisonné de Diplomatique' (Paris, 1774), says, p. 161, that in the first four centuries the title of Pope was usually given to Bishops indiscriminately. In the ninth century the Bishops of France were reprimanded by Pope Gregory IV. for addressing him as 'Papa.' In the eleventh century Pope Gregory VII. adopted the title 'Papa,' and refused it to all other Bishops. And in the thirteenth century the Popes united the title of Vicar of Christ to themselves, though it has been previously borne by other Bishops.

Newman, in his 'Essay on the Development of

[1] Vol. ii., p. 584.

Christian Doctrine,' states, p. 165: 'First the power of the Bishop awoke, then the power of the Pope.'

The Pope claims supremacy as the successor of St. Peter. But St. Peter himself claimed no such supremacy. Else how can we explain his not claiming that supremacy at the Council at Jerusalem, where St. James gave the judgment, ' Wherefore my sentence is' (Acts xv. 19). Would St. Paul have rebuked the 'Vicar of Christ'? (Gal. ii. 14).

We will end by quoting Bishop Wordsworth (' Letters to M. Goudon on the Destructive Character of the Church of Rome ') :

'So that, in fact, the primitive ages of the Church, the purest, the Apostolic times, did not hold that doctrine on which the cause of Rome's Christianity depends. Thus Rome is brought into the company of those heretics of whom Tertullian says they " were wont to say that the Apostles were not acquainted with all Christian doctrine or that they did not declare it fully to the world : not perceiving that by these assertions they exposed Christ Himself to obloquy for having chosen men who were either ill informed or else not honest." Our Lord Himself says (John xv. 26) : " All things that I have heard of My Father I have made known unto you." And John xiv. 26 : The Holy Spirit should teach them all things, and guide them into all truth, and bring all things to their remembrance, whatever He had said unto them. St. Paul, in Acts xx. 20-27, declares unto them "all the counsel of God"; and Gal. i. 8 : Though an angel from heaven preach unto them anything beside what he had preached unto them, and they had received from him, let him be accursed. So since it is acknowledged that the doctrine of the Pope's supremacy and infallibility was not developed in the Apostolic age, it cannot be any part of the "whole counsel of God," and as this doctrine is the foundation on which the whole Roman system is based, and since it is destructive of the only foundation which is laid (1 Cor. iii. 11), let the advocates of that system consider whether they are not liable to the anathema pronounced by St. Paul on all who teach anything as Christian doctrine besides what had been preached by him and received by the Church from him.'

The invocation of saints and of the Virgin Mary was introduced by P. Gnapheus of Antioch, about A.D. 470.

The supremacy of the Popes was initiated by Boniface III., about A.D. 600.

The Popes assumed the power of raising mortals to the dignity of saints, and making them objects of worship, in the ninth century.

Purgatory was not affirmed as a doctrine till A.D. 1140.

The two sacraments were multiplied into seven in the twelfth century.

The Cup, in the communion, was taken away from the laity by the Council of Constance, in A.D. 1416.

With these facts before us, how can we say that the 'Catholic Church is historically the same in personal identity and functions'? We have seen it is not the same either in the one or the other.

In the letter of January 20, 1854, the Bible and antiquity are to be put entirely aside, and the infallible teaching of the Pope is to stand in their place. We thought 'antiquity' was claimed as one of the Pope's strongholds; but it seems not. Of course, if the present Pope is infallible, the previous Popes have been so too. Let us glance at the history of a few of the Pope's predecessors.

But first we meet with a difficulty that cannot be surmounted, as we find that in 1400 there were no less than three Popes at the same time—Gregory XII., Alexander V., and Benedict XIII. Again in 1327 there were two Popes, bitterly hostile to each other—John XXII. and Nicholas V.—until at last the latter, deserted by his friends, saved his life by appearing before the former with a rope round his neck.

Alexander VI. was elected Pope in 1492. He was of the infamous family of the Borgias, and when a Cardinal had openly lived with a Roman lady named Vanezza, by whom he had four sons and one daughter. He first invited Charles VIII. of France to seize the kingdom of Naples, then entered into a treaty with the King of Naples, whose daughter married one of the Pope's sons, and begged for assistance from the Emperor Maximilian, and at the same time urged Ferdinand, King of Spain, to employ against the French the money subscribed in Spain for a crusade against the Turks; while, to add to his infamy, he proposed a secret treaty to the Sultan Bayazid. The Sultan offered three hundred thousand ducats and military assistance, provided the Pope would put to death the Sultan's brother, Prince Jem, who was then in Rome. These latter terms were agreed to.

Meanwhile Charles VIII. entered Rome. The Pope made peace with the French King, and surrendered Prince Jem to him, having previously given him a dose of poison. The Pope's daughter Lucretis had four husbands, from two of whom she was divorced, and the third she poisoned. She committed incest with both her brothers, the Duke of Gandia and Cardinal Cæsar Borgia, and on her showing preference for the former, he was slain by the latter. The Pope, after taking the side of the French in a new war against the Spaniards, which he had fomented, was at a loss for funds after the first defeats of the French. He consequently proposed to poison all the rich Cardinals, and afterwards seize their revenues. He sent several flasks of poisoned wine to the Cardinal of Corneto, in whose house they were to sup.

Strict orders were given that no person was to taste this wine; but the Pope and his son, Cardinal Cæsar, arriving early, and calling for some wine before supper, one of these flasks was opened. The Pope, feeling at once that he was poisoned, prevented his son from drinking as much as he himself had taken, and died in a few hours.

Pope Adrian VI. died in 1523 after a painful illness, during which the Cardinals and clergy of Rome openly prayed for his death, and on that event taking place, they erected a statue to his physician with the inscription 'Liberatori Patriæ.' Pope Adrian was buried in St. Peter's between Pius II. and Pius III., and on his tomb was written, 'Impius inter pios' (State Papers, Henry VIII.).

In celebration of the massacre of St. Bartholomew's Day, in 1672, a *Te Deum* was ordered by the Pope, and a silver medal with, on one side, an effigy of the reigning Pope and the inscription 'Gregorius XIII., Pont. Max. An. I.,' and on the other side a winged angel with a crucifix elevated in his right hand, and with a sword in his left stabbing a man, who, with a crowd, flies before him over heaps of dead bodies, and the inscription 'Ugonotorum strages.'

Cardinal (then Dr.) Newman sent a letter to the *Times* on this subject in September, 1872:

'You have lately, in your article on the massacre of St. Bartholomew's Day, thrown down a challenge to us on a most serious subject. I have no claim to speak for my brethren, but I speak in default of better men. No Pope can make evil good. No Pope has any power over those eternal moral principles which God has imprinted on our hearts and consciences. If any Pope has, with his eyes open, approved treachery or cruelty, let those defend that Pope who can. If any Pope at any time has had his mind so occupied with the desirableness of the Church's triumph over her enemies as to be dead to the treacherous and savage acts by which that triumph was achieved, let those who feel disposed say that in such conduct he acted up to his high office of maintaining justice and showing mercy. Craft and cruelty, and whatever is base and wicked, have a sure Nemesis, and eventually strike the heads of those who are guilty of them. Whether in matter of fact Gregory XIII. had a share in the guilt of the St. Bartholomew massacre must be proved to me before I believe it. It is commonly said in his defence that he had an untrue, one-sided account of the matter presented to him, and acted on misinformation. This involves a question of fact, which historians must decide. But even if they decide against the Pope, his infallibility is in no respect compromised. Infallibility is not impeccability; even Caiaphas prophesied, and Gregory XIII. was not quite a Caiaphas.'

This letter gives an instance of the manner in which

Roman Catholics, and more especially the recent perverts, treat history. The 'historian' to whom we are referred is the Roman Catholic Church itself, as Manning told Robert Wiberforce. But we need not go into that question. We stand by the Pope's acts after the event. Did Dr. Newman know of the existence of this medal? If he did not, he should have informed himself, before committing himself. No 'untrue one-sided account' or 'misinformation' can explain away the device or the inscription on the medal.

Can such as these be the infallible teachers of the Church? Can these be the 'Vicars of Christ'?

We cannot be in the least surprised at finding Robert Wilberforce 'scandalized with St. Alphonsus.' No honest man on reading his works, and more especially the treatise on 'Equivocation on Oaths,' could well be otherwise than scandalized. How can 'certain equivocations even firmed with an oath' be truth? Manning himself, in another letter, calls them 'execrable ambiguities.'

Again, in the letter of February 28, 1854:

'You say quite truly, "St. Alphonsus does not say that you may lie, but he says that is truth which is a lie."'

This sentence gives the whole case away. You must not steal, but if you do steal somebody else's money, it is no theft.

Why, if 'the most could be that the congregation which examined St. Alphonsus' works failed of their due diligence, and that St. Alphonsus is open to censure,' does Manning still support his propositions? It is not a question simply of blaming the congregation which examined the works. The works were not published yesterday. Every year those works are uncondemned by the Index Expurgatorium renders the Pope and all his entourage responsible, as they have full power to forbid any book to their adherents, clerical or lay. Why was Liguori canonized? Pius VII. publicly approved of his works in 1803, and Leo XII. gave a golden medal to the editor of Liguori's works, together with the brief, on February 19, 1825. Of course, we have the excuse made, 'Who knows St. Alphonsus' meaning?' Just in the same way we were asked, 'Who knows the history of the Catholic Church?' In diplomacy words are used to conceal intentions; we may regret the fact, but under no conditions should they ever be so used in a matter of religion.

What can we think of the prayer that concludes the letter of February 28, 1854?

'Most sincerely do I pray that you may be delivered from the whole system of insincerity by which you are surrounded.'

On which side lay the insincerity? In the letter of May 19, 1854, in what sense do the miracles and legends present themselves to the mind of the poorest Catholic? Are they not taught to believe in them implicitly? What of the miracles at Lourdes at the present day, or of the numerous pilgrimages which all bring grist to the mill of the Pope or the priest? What of the relics? Are they all suppositions?

CHAPTER VIII.

'IN the concluding paragraph of Manning's Diary, 1851 to 1854, is the following somewhat singular but candid self-revelation: "I am conscious of a desire to be in such a position (1) as I had in times past; (2) as my present circumstances imply by the act of others; (3) as my friends think me fit for; (4) as I feel my own faculties tend to. But, God being my helper, I will not seek it by the lifting of a finger, or the speaking of a word. If it is ever to be, it shall be (1) either by the invitation of superiors, or (2) by the choice of others. And then I desire to remove the final determination from my own will to that of others, according to the resolution of last year." [1]

'Cardinal Manning thought it necessary to append to the Diary of 1854 the following explanatory footnote, dated August 5, 1883: "The people and papers had been making a Bishop of me." [2]

[1] Vol. ii., p. 17.   [2] Vol. ii., p. 17.

We shall see in due course how he kept his resolution.

'Conscious of his aptitude for administrative work, Manning lost no time in making himself useful to Cardinal Wiseman. . . . In connection with Catholic chaplains in the Crimea during the war, with Wiseman's sanction, he entered into communication with the War Department.'[1]

The first step on the road to promotion is, naturally, to ingratiate himself with his superiors. This is neither 'lifting a finger' nor 'speaking a word,' but it has the same effect. It is at least curious to find the convert of 1851 taking such an important political part in the organization of the Roman Catholic Church in England as early as 1854.

'In the spring of 1853, all the English in Rome interested in Church matters, or moved by curiosity to see and hear the celebrated preacher, crowded into the church. Manning once remarked: "Faces familiar to me when I was preaching in Rome, I often recognised again when I was preaching in London. Many of those people who heard me preach in Rome for the first time, came to me in London in their religious doubts and difficulties, seeking either comfort or instruction, and many of them I have received into the Church."'[2]

We wonder whether they were instructed on the

[1] Vol. ii., p. 51. [2] Vol. ii., p. 23.

same lines that Robert Wilberforce was in the letters. Was St. Alphonsus explained in the same way, or was he quietly ignored? How were they instructed to regard miracles and legends?

Manning wrote to Robert Wilberforce on April 1, 1856:

'... God knows what it has cost me to be a priest, and to do the work of a priest, and to bear the name of a priest, here in the midst of kindred and old friends, and the world in which I lived before. No one, I believe, had more sensitive shrinking from this peculiar stage of trials. I have thought that you seemed to think that I entered upon this with more willingness or less suffering than you. It was only that I believed that my salvation probably depends upon pressing onward in correspondence with every motion of grace that could have brought me to it.'[1]

This letter is worthy of St. Alphonsus himself; there is not a word of truth in it.

In the autobiographical note (already quoted), on his entering the Church of Rome, Manning said:

'I fully believed I should never do more than become a priest, about which I never doubted or ever wavered.'

Had Manning this 'sensitive shrinking,' why did he not follow Newman's lead? Newman had never pushed himself to the front, but had settled down

[1] Vol. ii., p. 46.

quietly at the Oratory at Birmingham. Did the 'entering into correspondence with the War Department' within three years of joining the Church of Rome indicate 'sensitive shrinking'?

Mr. Purcell tells us :

' Had he [Manning] desired to become a Jesuit, the long noviciate—which would not have been relaxed in his favour—would have kept him for many years out of sight and out of public work ; but this delay would not have suited Wiseman's views nor Manning's own wishes.'[1]

Robert Wilberforce died of fever at Rome before he had been ordained priest.

We give next a letter from Cardinal Wiseman to Monsignor Talbot, the Pope's Chamberlain. It will give a good illustration of the 'Unity' among the Roman Catholics themselves. The subject of the letter forms the commencement of the internal squabbles which lasted throughout Wiseman's life and the greater part of Manning's. It is dated January 16, 1853 :

' Here is a sad business about to happen. The accompanying correspondence will explain it.[2] I do not wish to do more at present than ask you to read it, and make known its contents to the Holy Father.

[1] Vol. ii., p. 58.
[2] 'Correspondence between Cardinal Wiseman and Dr. Grant, Bishop of Southwark, on the Division of Church Property and Trust Funds consequent on the Division of the two Dioceses.

The very idea of a suffragan of the new Hierarchy, almost within a year, going off to Rome to carry thither a cause against his Metropolitan, and that that one should be Dr. Grant, *homo pacis miræ*, put at Southwark because he was my friend, is fraught with scandal. But I regret to say it, after the first few weeks that he was in England, he became estranged, kept aloof, and made those men his counsellors who had always favoured and headed the old party against me before he came, and finally chose for his Chapter those very men who, through the disturbance of the " Papal Aggression," were suspected of being the confederates of Lord John Russell, alluded to in his speech, and authors of the letter signed " A Catholic Priest," in the *Times*. I foresaw all along what would take place, and there has been no cordiality, no sympathy; months pass without his calling on me, and every little complaint, every discontent has gone to him. . . . You are aware, too, when I was made Cardinal, his Holiness, so far from thinking my income too large for my present position, most generously and munificently added to it. Providence has assisted me in other ways, or I should have been in straits. . . . But you must be tired with this unfortunate affair— Bishops quarrelling about *meum et tuum, frigida verba*. What I hope is, that the scandal of a Bishop starting off for Rome on such an errand, and dragging his Metropolitan after him (for if he goes, I suppose I must), may be prevented. Let him be desired to send his case in writing—let me see it, and I will reply in full, and let the Holy Father decide between us. I trust the Holy Father will take this into consideration and *into his own hands*. I fear Dr. Grant may have already written elsewhere. I may remark that many of our Trusts are most difficult to unravel, and are obliged to be kept most secret for fear of the Mortmain laws, and obligations for Masses, so that I cannot even have new deeds or transfers made, as by registering them, necessary to make them legal, we might endanger the whole property.'[1]

Here is a truly edifying picture of a Church that is 'in harmony and obedience to the truth, and the will of our Divine Lord'; that alone is 'in the sphere and guidance of the Divine Spirit'; that has 'the Divine life and Divine reality in its acts'; that has no 'false view of moral probation'; that is not a 'whole system of insincerity'; nor is 'human, fragmentary, and a dishonour to our Lord and to the redeemed intelligence.'

We have the first view here of that intrigue in the Roman Catholic Church in which Manning afterwards showed himself such an expert.

How can that Church be said to be 'in harmony and obedience to the truth, and the will of our Divine Lord,' when it distinctly disobeys His command, 'Render to Cæsar the things that are Cæsar's'?

[1] Vol. ii., p. 56.

The first duty the Roman Catholic Church inculcates is obedience, and yet we find that same Church setting such an example.

There is one other important sentence in this letter: 'I trust the Holy Father will take this into consideration and *into his own hands.*'

This at once proves that the responsibility for the works of St. Alphonsus de Liguori did not rest only on the congregation that passed his books, but was also shared by the Pope.

'In the autumn of this year (1856) Cardinal Wiseman appointed Manning Diocesan Inspector of Schools.'[1]

Manning wished to found an Order of the 'Oblates of St. Charles' in London, and travelled to Genoa to obtain full details of the rules of the Order, and thus writes to Cardinal Wiseman from Genoa, on December 15, 1856:

'The Archbishop of [Milan] received us very kindly, and has given us two relics of the blood of St. Charles. There was no portion of the body to be obtained.'[2]

In what 'sense' did Manning regard these relics? And in what 'sense' were the future Oblates to be instructed as to these wonderful relics? It seems extraordinary, when we know how relics multiplied, that a portion of the body could not have been 'invented.'

[1] Vol. ii., p. 54. [2] Vol. ii., p. 61.

In the Journal of 1879, speaking of these same Oblates, Cardinal Manning says:

'There remains one work—I mean the Oblates of St. Charles. It was at once sorely tried by a very formidable opposition. It was confirmed by the trial. If it had not been God's will, it would not have been assailed; and if it had not been His work, it could never have endured the assault. It grew steadily, and having survived all trial from without, it was more perilously tried, as I foretold, from within. Minds without humility destroyed their own stability and that of others. They sowed division, which vexed, lowered, and saddened the community.'[1]

The above remarks apply to any work and any system. Mohammedanism was 'at once tried by a very formidable opposition. It was confirmed by the trial. If it had not been God's will, it would not have been assailed; and if it had not been His work, it could never have endured the assault. It grew steadily, and having survived all trial from without, it was more perilously tried from within,' in the split between the Sunnites and the Shiites. But Cardinal Manning would hardly have approved of this. But he (and too many others of different religions do the same) was only judging the 'work' himself, instead of leaving it to the Final Judgment.

Was he unknowingly giving us a short character of

[1] Vol. ii., p. 73.

himself? 'Minds without humility destroyed their own stability and that of others.' That sentence seems exactly to describe his characteristics in the Church of England; and during his career in the Church of Rome, as we shall see, he fulfilled the remaining portion: 'sowed division, which vexed, lowered, and saddened the community.'

In one of his autobiographical notes, Cardinal Manning, in speaking of his visits to Rome for the purpose of obtaining the Pope's sanction to the founding of the Oblates of St. Charles in London, and subsequently, as the official agent of Cardinal Wiseman, said: 'These visits made me known to the chief official personages, the ruling Cardinals at Propaganda, and brought me into intimate relations with the Pope. All this led to my becoming what I now am.'[1]

We are told during his life in the Church of England, 'It was in the nature of his cautious and forecasting temperament to study betimes the lie of the land through which his pathway led.'[2]

Had he not done so in this case? Did he not well know that the founding *and ruling* this Order in London would not only give him a position of trust, but would also bring him into contact with the ruling powers in Rome? Was this work, then, undertaken for God or for ambition? What of the entry in the Journal of 1879, quoted above?

[1] Vol. ii., p. 2.   [2] Vol. i., p. 172.

Manning early took up the position of agent, official or otherwise, of Cardinal Wiseman, as we find him writing from Rome under date January 7, 1857 :

'In a day or two I hope to see Cardinal Barnabò (Provost of Propaganda) again, and I will take care to put him in possession of the truth of these matters, which are little enough, but mischievous and vexatious. I am very sorry that you should be troubled with them, but they are the ecclesiastical gnats which I find to infest chiefly high places.'[1]

The next letter has a further bearing on the great question of 'Unity,' and is dated from Rome, January 21, 1857 :

'. . . I suppose it is the office of the Catholic Church to "gather of all kinds," and to assimilate all diversities, and to suffer much internal trouble in doing so. Certainly we are in a continual fever of criticisms and personal oppositions. And being a society numerically small in England, it is like a small town in which tongues are, if not more busy, yet always more audible and troublesome than in a great city. It has seemed to me that we have a great plague of tongues upon us, and it sometimes gives me much disquiet lest I should in any way or degree (of which I am not conscious, for I detest it) have done the same. And if there be one subject which more than another seems to me odious and immoral, it is the

[1] Vol. ii., p. 62.

comparison of gifts, or cultivation, or services rendered to the Church of God by the two classes which ought to be indistinguishable in the unity of the faith.'[1]

While Manning was still in Rome, the Pope appointed him Provost of the Chapter of Westminster.

'Cardinal Wiseman, out of prudence or a love of peace, had intended to make Dr. Maguire, on Dr. Whitty's resignation, head of the Chapter; but in his heart rejoiced that, without consulting him, Pope Pius IX. had taken the appointment into his own hands.'[2]

Manning wrote to Cardinal Wiseman from Rome, April 8, 1857:

'To-day a rescript of Propaganda came to me, not in the tenour of your Eminence's kind letter of some time ago, but of the provostship. I cannot but believe that there has been some departure from your intention in this; remembering our conversation about Dr. Maguire, to whom I shall rejoice to transfer what I think must have been intended for him. I have not yet seen Dr. Whitty or Monsignor Talbot, or spoken on the subject to anyone, except at Propaganda, when I first heard of it. But I will see them to-morrow, and will wait here or not until your answer can come, according as they may advise.'[3]

Was Manning, perhaps, afraid that this provostship might stand in the way of the bishopric which had

[1] Vol. ii., p. 63.   [2] Vol. ii., p. 76.   [3] Vol. ii., p. 75.

been so much talked about for the last three years? Had not Manning been made aware by his friend, Monsignor Talbot, that this appointment had been made by the Pope without consultation with Cardinal Wiseman?

The bargain with the Pope was now, no doubt, fulfilled, as Mr. Purcell tells us:

'In the Provostship of Westminster Manning enjoyed an office equivalent to that of Chichester. Moreover, his field of action was larger by far, for it included Rome, the centre of the Catholic world, and all that Rome implies in work and worship; and since evil must needs exist in high places or low, Catholic or non-Catholic, all that Rome in times of turmoil implies as source and centre of ambition and intrigue. . . . "It is well," as Manning in a letter to his friend at the Vatican, Monsignor Talbot, wrote, "that the Protestant world does not know how our work is hindered by domestic strife."'[1]

The Protestant world found out Rome more than three hundred years ago, but it is refreshing to find a Roman Catholic stigmatizing Rome as 'the source and centre of ambition and intrigue.' Protestants have done so for centuries.

Six days later Manning again addresses Cardinal Wiseman:

'Since I first heard of it, I have been going through

[1] Vol. ii., p. 80.

a good deal, arising in part from sensitiveness and a dread of leaving the quiet and retirement which, after many years of trial, I have had in the last six. One thing gives me comfort, which is the hope that I may be of more use to you and better able to relieve you of some among your many lesser employments.'[1]

Again a letter according to the maxims of St. Alphonsus. What quiet and retirement had Manning had? His life in those six years had been spent either in London or in Rome, and he had been pushing himself into prominence in every available manner.

'Speaking of Manning in those early days of his Catholic life, the President of Ushaw said: "I hate that man, he is such a forward piece."'[2]

'Manning's promotion was not, perhaps, the cause of, but the signal for, letting loose the long-pent-up waters of strife. His growing intimacy and influence with Wiseman was resented by some on personal grounds, by others for public or ecclesiastical reasons. This intimacy, however, arose just too late to prevent the greatest mistake in Wiseman's life—the appointment of Dr. Errington as his coadjutor, with right of succession. At the time of this unlucky appointment, Manning's attention was absorbed by his work with the Jesuits at Farm Street. His mind at that time was, perhaps, not made up as to the policy, or line of

[1] Vol. ii., p. 66. [2] Vol. ii., p. 76.

action to be pursued. He was still feeling his way. . . . It was Manning's hand that lighted up the smouldering flame, either by accident, or by over-zeal on behalf of his new community; for he placed his Oblates—of course, with the concurrence of Cardinal Wiseman—in St. Edmund's, the seminary of Westminster and Southwark. Bishop Grant resented this act as an unlawful intrusion; so did Dr. Errington.'[1]

The idea of a subaltern dictating to his Colonel is rather comical. How could Manning, then a newly-joined convert, interfere in the appointment of a coadjutor Bishop and the right of succession to the highest position in the Roman Catholic Church in England?

'He was still feeling his way.'

When, during the whole course of his life, did he cease doing that? Certainly not during his life in the Church of England, and, as we shall see, not at any time during his life in the Church of Rome.

We must acquit him of 'lighting up the smouldering flame by accident.' His 'cautious and forecasting temperament' was a guarantee against that, and our next extract is a further proof:

'. . . This prolonged struggle — in which Manning in reality was the prime mover—to deprive Dr. Errington of his right of succession to Westminster.'[2]

[1] Vol. ii., p. 76.   [2] Vol. ii., p. 80.

Manning had everything to gain, and nothing to lose, by fomenting squabbles among the Bishops. The succession of Dr. Errington, the man who 'hated such a forward piece,' to Cardinal Wiseman would have been fatal to Manning's chance of a bishopric.

'No sooner had Monsignor Searle discovered that Manning was working at York Place and in Rome for the removal of Dr. Errington, than he entered into active relations with the Bishops, and with the coadjutor himself, warning him of what he described as " Manning's intrigue." '[1]

Here is a glorious instance of 'Unity'—Wiseman and Manning arrayed against the rest of the Bishops. But Manning was equal to the occasion.

'It did not require much time or trouble on the part of a man of such infinite tact and skill as Manning to gain supreme influence over Monsignor Talbot. If Monsignor Talbot had the ear of the Pope, the tongue which spoke in whispers was not Talbot's.'[2]

The conspiracy, after the exercise of this so-called 'tact and skill,' was successful.

'The removal of Dr. Errington, by the supreme act of the Pope, was a stretch of Papal authority, not easily forgotten on either side. It was in truth what Pope Pius IX. called it: "a *coup d' état* of the Lord God." '[3]

[1] Vol. ii., p. 83. [2] Vol. ii., p. 87. [3] Vol. ii., p. 95.

The 'whispers' had been effectual. But what can we think of this blasphemous statement of the Pope? Can these be the words of the Vicar of Christ? One of his predecessors, Boniface VIII., described Christianity as 'a lucrative fable.'

Was Pope Pius IX. of the same opinion? Was it because the Pope, at his coronation, was carried in his chair and seated on the altar with his feet resting on the altar, that he used these words? 'And as God, seated in the temple of God, showing that he is God (2 Thess. ii. 4).

What are we to think of the following extract from *The Guardian*, of June 17, 1896, under the heading 'France'?

'When, in his book " Le Christianisme et les Temps Présents,' the late Bishop of Laval wrote that only half of our Lord was present in the Holy Eucharist, and that the other half was in the Vatican, that "the Pope is the second form of the Real Presence of Jesus Christ in the Church," that "Jesus Christ present in the Vatican could alone sustain a Church and render it infallible," most people regarded it as the rash utterance of an enthusiast. But it would really seem that these wild effusions are growing into dogmatic formulas. The Bishop of Bayonne, who at his appointment was even regarded with suspicion in clerical circles as too liberal, has just paid his usual *ad limina* visit to Rome, and therefore his words at such a time must be well weighed. Before he set out he issued the usual pastoral, in which he wrote: "We will say to the Pope, in all submission, even as to the Spirit of God on the Day of Pentecost (Whitsunday prayer, Missal): O Father of those who are in need, Whose word enlightens and comforts — *Pater pauperum, consolator optime, O Lux beatissime*—cleanse us from our faults, uphold our weakness, heal our diseases, make straight our ways, make us obedient to your commands, enfold us in your holy fervour." And again, on his return, the Bishop preached on Whit Sunday in his cathedral, and said (official gazette of the diocese): 'The Son of God continues really present in the Church by His own Sacrament, the Eucharist. The Eucharist of the Holy Spirit, which renders Him always present under the corporeal substance, is the infallible Pope, *Os orbis*. It has been said most justly, that the Pope is the Ego of the Church.... The Pope, the visible personification of the Spirit of God, ... The Pope, the Incarnation of the Holy Ghost."'

'Objective worship' is at the root of it all.

CHAPTER IX.

WE now have the task of unravelling the plots of the two allies, Manning in London and Talbot in Rome, and we shall see at the same time the effect of the 'whispers.'

The following, from Manning to Talbot, written from St. Mary's, Bayswater, under date August 18, 1859, brings a serious charge against the original Roman Catholics, as distinguished from the recent converts:

'. . . I am resolved not to speak on the subject unless forced, and then I will simply relate a series of facts, which have come to my knowledge, as to the state of practice and faith among them, both priests and people, who claim to be "Old Catholics." I look upon them as one of the greatest evils in England, and if it gain head I believe the Church, as far as it can be, will be paralysed in the very moment of its growth and expansion.'[1]

Where, then, is the boasted 'Unity' of the Roman

[1] Vol. ii., p. 98.

Catholic Church, even in matters of faith? Again, on September 17, 1859, Manning writes:

'We are in a crisis in which, if the spirit represented by Dr. Errington, Dr. Grant, and Searle prevail, the work of the Church in England will be done by the religious, and the secular clergy will, for a generation to come, lose ground in all the points most essential for their action upon the people in England. They will continue to administer the Sacrament to the almost exclusively Irish population now in England, but the work and mission of the Church as contemplated by the Holy Father in the Hierarchy, and as demanded by the state of England, and, I will say, by the manifest will of God shown in His providential acts, will be thrown back for a whole generation.'[1]

The effect of this letter must have been to poison the mind of the Pope against Dr. Errington, Bishop Grant, and Canon Searle. Manning had already triumphed over Dr. Errington, Bishop Grant was a sturdy opponent of Manning from the beginning, and Canon Searle, who had for years been Wiseman's most intimate and confidential adviser, was to be ousted from this position—and the first step was to blacken his character at Rome.

Talbot writes to Manning, from the Vatican, on January 29, 1860:

'I am attacked also, in the meanest manner, for

[1] Vol. ii., p. 99.

supporting the Cardinal [Wiseman]. My antagonist holds it as a principle that everything but actual sin is lawful to defend his cause. I have known him to suggest the shabbiest acts in order, as he said, to do good. . . . But you must remain firm and not flinch, because some hard things will be said against you, and are being said at this moment. It is remarkable that the attack upon three of the leading converts should coincide—yourself, Newman, and Faber. It was to be expected, so that I only hope that the converts will remain firm under their persecution, and I have no doubt that they will triumph in the end. Their zeal, their energy, their superiority in many respects to the old stock, is the cause of the jealousy.'[1]

Can Manning complain of 'the principle that everything but actual sin is lawful to defend his cause'? How does his great teacher, St. Alphonsus de Liguori, treat the matter? He says a sin committed for the cause of religion is not a sin at all.

Did Manning stop at actual sin, even to gain his own ends? Was the ninth commandment never broken by these two allies—who certainly cannot be acquitted of having resorted to the 'shabbiest acts'?

What of the following letter from Manning to Talbot, under date August 17, 1860:

'From one very competent informant I hear that the staff of St. Edmund's is worse than ever. I am

[1] Vol. ii., p. 124.

told . . . and that smoking goes on contrary to the known rule: that H. Y. was barred out of a room where the boys were drinking and smoking; that the Cardinal is "detested" by the boys, and Dr. Grant in great repute; this is the work of Dr. Grant and his Southwark friends.'[1]

The first story Manning has to tell is erased from the letter, and as 'smoking and drinking' are mentioned, we must conclude that the accusation must be a much more serious one, to warrant this erasure.

Manning again writes, on September 14, 1860:

'. . . I hear the Bishops spare the Cardinal [Wiseman], and fall upon you and me. We, I am glad to say, are his conductors. I dare say we shall both hear more of it, and shall have to look to our tackle.'[2]

Here is a bold acknowledgment that he and Talbot were at the bottom of all the intrigues. We mentioned it before, but here is proof under Manning's own hand.

On the same day Manning wrote:

'. . . So long as the Cardinal lives I do not anticipate any great attempt to make a reaction, but, if he were taken away, I think you and I and those who have stood together in this contest, will have to look about us. It is of the first importance that we should be foresighted, and that we should keep the Propaganda fully informed of everything. It would be of

[1] Vol. ii., p. 124.   [2] Vol. ii., p. 134.

vital importance that there should always be in Rome someone to do the work you do now. Humanly speaking, those whom God has brought into the Church would have been mistrusted and suspected and misrepresented for a generation to come, if you had not been upon the spot. All this is very sad. Thank God the Protestants do not know that half our time and strength is wasted in contests *inter domesticos fidei*. We have two great antagonists, the Protestant Association of Bayswater and the Chapter of Westminster. This is very grievous and must displease God.'[1]

It is a blasphemous assumption to drag in the name of God in such a cause. Did Manning think the intrigue, the low trickery, the backbiting, were acceptable to God?

But perhaps he only meant the 'Lord God,' or, in other words, the 'Pope.'

There is no fear that Manning will be 'misrepresented for a generation to come.' He stands out boldly in colours designed by himself, and is a fit type of a pervert, and of the Roman Catholic Church in its political and ecclesiastical character.

On December 13, 1860, Manning writes:

'... If Searle were gone we should have no more [contention]; but his jealousy of everyone would be laughable if it were not troublesome to others. I am

[1] Vol. ii., p. 100.

convinced that he compromises the Cardinal with all sorts of people, and the Cardinal's house will never be accessible as it should be as long as he is there.'[1]

The plot against Canon Searle thickens, and Talbot wrote to Manning on the same day (December 13):

'I agree with you more and more, and see that until the old generation of Bishops and priests is removed—to heaven, I hope, because they are good men—no great progress of religion can be expected in England. I have watched the religious movement which exists there for twenty years, and now that I can calmly and coolly look back to what has taken place, I can see how the older progress in piety, in Roman spirit, in conversions, etc., has been in spite of the rulers of the Church and the priests who used to be looked upon as oracles ... No, it has been prejudice, jealousy! The priests in England, and the Bishops, too, are good men, but prejudice and jealousy are the failings of good men; all the religious Orders have them in a high degree.'[2]

This letter advocates a very clean sweep—no less than the removal of the whole of the 'old generation of Bishops and priests.'

It must be noted that those who are so anxious, as Talbot tells Manning he is, in a letter dated June 12, 1859, 'for the greater glory of God, the exaltation of the Church, and the salvation of souls,'[3] are somewhat

---

[1] Vol. ii., p. 134.   [2] Vol. ii., p. 101.   [3] Vol. ii., p. 99.

indefinite as to the state of those they impose as 'spiritual directors' upon the members of their Church. Surely, in the 'to heaven, I hope,' the latter part was superfluous.

If the shepherd is a castaway, what are the prospects of the sheep? The latter part of the letter contains a stronger condemnation than could have been passed by any Protestant.

On January 3, 1861, Talbot wrote:

'The note of Lord John Russell is the most unprincipled document that ever was written by a Minister of any civilized Court. He maintains in it the principle that the end justifies the means, and that evil can be done if those who do it have good intentions —that robbery and rebellion are lawful.'[1]

On what other principle has Rome ever acted? Lord John Russell could only be accused by Roman Catholics of acting on the teaching of St. Alphonsus de Liguori. In how many cases has Rome stirred up rebellion in this country alone? But, of course, the whole matter assumes a different aspect when their own possessions are at stake. How many Bulls of the Popes, the so-called Vicars of Christ, can be included in the category of the 'most unprincipled documents that ever were written by a Minister of any civilized Court'? We are thankful for the last epithet. We remember when Manning asked Milanesi,

[1] Vol. ii., p. 164.

one of the members of the Circolo Romano, 'why Acatholic countries were in advance, and Catholic in the rear of civilization, he admitted the fact.'[1] Now we see that it is not Roman Catholic countries only, but the Court of Rome and the infallible Pope that are in the rear of civilization.

We shall have occasion to allude to this again.

Manning writes on January 5, 1861:

'The Protestant political spirit is very confident and overbearing, encouraged by the state of Italy and the belief that England is at last succeeding in overthrowing the Pope's temporal power and influence over Catholic nations. Also, the volunteer movement has taught the Government that it need not depend on Ireland for an army. My belief is that the Catholics in this country have not been so weak in politics for fifty years. . . . All these things would be of no moment if we were united among ourselves; but, unhappily, as you say, we are tormented by prejudice and jealousy. If we yield to it, all the gain we have made is in risk, and much will be lost. The incapacity of most of the Catholics to deal with the altered state of the Church in England is every day more apparent, and I fear many of them prefer the old state of the Church, when it hardly ventured out of its inactivity, to its present conflict with the English people. You say I am in proximate occasions of coming to Rome. I

[1] Vol. i., p. 388.

confess I should enjoy very much to be there at this time. It is a great grace to be near the Vicar of Christ when the world is upon him; and if I could be in two places at once, as the Saints and the birds, I would come.'[1]

The 'conflict with the English people' was not on a question of religion at all, but simply political. It was only the question of the temporal power of the Pope.

Imagine the Vicar of Christ clutching his ill-gotten wealth, and Manning talking of its being 'a great grace to be near him' while he is doing so!

We must not, at this juncture, forget what Cardinal Manning said in 1887 (as we have already quoted), as to the cause of the success of the Revolution in Italy, viz., 'the laxity of morals in the clergy, seculars and regulars.'[2]

Manning does not explain how the 'birds' can be in two places at once. Did he allude to Sir Boyle Roche's bull in the Irish House of Commons in 1792? As to the 'Saints,' no doubt Manning was alluding to St. John Joseph of the Cross, who was canonized on Trinity Sunday, May 26, 1839, and of whom it is said, 'His frequent ravishment from the earth and suspension in the air was a well-known occurrence,' and, 'nor was that singular prerogative

[1] Vol. ii., p. 163.   [2] Vol. i., p. 386, note.

denied him, which God's Saints have sometimes possessed, of appearing in two places at once.'[1]

Cardinal Wiseman had a serious illness during the winter of 1860-61, and Manning thus writes to his co-conspirator on February 1, 1861:

'... One thing is certain, that the Southwark people are busy; and I am told that Searle has often been there during the time that he has been at Leyton, and that without letting the Cardinal know that he was in London. Also I hear that Dr. Grant has set his nuns to pray that he may not be removed to Beverley. I am only desirous, first, that all this should be known to Propaganda, and next, that no more than its real importance should be given to it.'[2]

Again, on March 21, 1861:

'While I was there Mgr. Searle provoked a collision, which will give you a sample of what is passing. Three months ago Dr. Ullathorne wrote to me twice, and came to me once, saying that the Cardinal was reviving the old question about the funds of the Midland District, and claiming money as due to him; and he, Dr. Ullathorne, intended to refer the case to Propaganda. I immediately saw that such a course would be most injurious to the Cardinal, both here and in Rome, for reasons both you and I know, and I felt

[1] 'Lives of the Saints, whose canonization took place Trinity Sunday, 1839,' p. 150.
[2] Vol. ii., p. 102.

convinced it was not the Cardinal's doing. On the first opportunity I asked him. He disclaimed all such intention, and said that nothing would induce him to revive the old variances. It seemed that I was right. . . . The disclaimer of the Cardinal, through me, was then written to Searle. . . . He began upon it curtly to-day. I said that I believed that I had accurately repeated the Cardinal's words. This he denied. I then said that the Cardinal ought to be the interpreter of his own meaning, and if he said I was inaccurate, I should at once say that I was mistaken. He then began by saying that my writing to Dr. Ullathorne was not "straightforward." I then felt he had passed his limits; and I told him that I had for two years considered his conduct in circumventing and undermining me, both in the Chapter and out of it, as not straightforward. He then said I ought to have spoken first to him. I answered that I owed him no relations; that I had a duty to the Cardinal and none to him. He then asked whether I considered I had a right to judge of questions between Bishops. I said, Certainly, if one is my own, whom I see being compromised in a way to do him great harm, and if the other brings the case to me. This is a sample of what we said—with much heat, I believe, on both sides: certainly on mine, for I was very angry at the whole affair. I found afterwards, from the Cardinal, that I had with perfect accuracy reported his words; that he fully saw the danger of reviving such a discussion here and in Rome, and that he would rather give up everything than allow it to be revived. Now I told the Cardinal openly that I had been very angry and had spoken with great warmth. And I could see, in the way he listened, that he was not sorry for it. I must therefore express what I have long felt, and for distinct reasons known to me, that Searle assumes too much, and that, in the weakened state of the Cardinal's health and nerves, he is overborne by Searle's assumption. This has already been said to me by a layman and professional attendant of the Cardinal's—a friend of Searle's, but a man of delicate feeling and sense of what is due to the Cardinal. But this you will kindly not quote. Now I have written this because it is well you should know how things are. Here is the Cardinal liable to be involved in a controversy with one of his suffragans about money and an old feud, and to be delated once more to Rome. I see no cure to this but putting some restraint on Mgr. Searle. . . . Since I wrote thus far I have had a conversation with one of the Cardinal's oldest and best friends—a layman—who has confirmed all I have said of Searle. It is my deliberate judgment that Searle's rude and overbearing manners have intimidated the Cardinal, and that his state of nervous depression puts him more than ever in his power. I feel, too, that the funds and the trusts of the diocese ought to be known to some two new persons—otherwise Searle will be left in sole possession, and the Cardinal's successor will be in a false position. . . . I wish I could see you, and I would come to Rome, but I do not like to leave the Cardinal, and he evidently does not like my leaving him ; and in truth I wish to be on the spot to keep things straight, for, if anything happens, I am resolved to carry it through. I will not allow anything which is contrary to the Cardinal's will or peace.'[1]

What a marvellous picture of the boasted ' Unity !' If Searle had been 'circumventing and undermining' Manning, surely, from what we have seen, it must have been done in self-defence. Searle, as we have said before, had been Wiseman's factotum. He had had charge for years of all funds and trusts, and not in Wiseman's present diocese only, but when he was Bishop in 'the Midlands.' Of all these matters Manning was kept in profound ignorance. *Hinc illæ lachrymæ*, and the proposal that two new persons should be appointed, of whom, of course, Manning would have been one.

Manning was really urging Talbot to obtain Searle's recall to Rome. That was the only practical way in which 'some restraint' could be put on him. He could then have been sent to a sphere of work in some other part of the world.

[1] Vol. ii., p. 103.

We have no doubt that if the 'layman and professional attendant of the Cardinal's, a friend of Searle's,' had expressed his real opinion, he would have forbidden either Manning or Searle to trouble the Cardinal at all at such a time with their trifling quarrels.

CHAPTER X.

ON June 18, 1861, Talbot wrote to Manning:
'... A great deal too much talk at Rome has been made about some expressions you made use of in your "Lectures on Antichrist," in which you said that Rome would some day return to Paganism. I have traced the origin of the ill-natured things said to the Irish College. I am told that it has been reported even to Propaganda. Although I am sorry you did make use of expressions in your lectures, yet I cannot attribute the animus manifested against you to zeal for the greater glory of God, and the salvation of souls. You may be certain that prejudice and jealousy are the root of the unkind things said about you. This you must expect. More you rise in England, more enemies will set themselves against you to criticize all you do, so that I recommend you to be constantly on your guard.'[1]

Again, on July 6, 1861:
'I think the affair about your lectures on Antichrist

[1] Vol. ii., p. 154

has been settled satisfactorily. It was an intrigue of your enemies to injure you in Rome. I wrote a long letter to Cardinal Bò on the subject, explaining the nature of the lectures, and attributing what had been said about them to a certain party in England, who act more from motives of prejudice and jealousy than from zeal for the salvation of souls and greater glory of God. As I wrote in virtue of my being Consulter of Propaganda, I received an official answer from the secretary, Monsignor Capalti, to the effect that your "Lectures on the Temporal Sovereignty of the Popes and the Present Crisis of the Holy See, tested by Prophecy" had been carefully examined by Propaganda, and approved of, though some statements were considered as inaccurate. Monsignor Capalti expressed regret at the prophecy which you have introduced that the City of the Popes would relapse into Paganism, and become the city of Antichrist. This statement Monsignor Capalti held to be inopportune. Besides, now I am having translated your most admirable sermons on the "Latter Glories of the Holy See," which I consider to be the best publication on the subject, so that I shall have them printed, and send a number of copies to Propaganda. All this shows how careful you must be, as you have enemies in every quarter, not merely amongst the old Catholics, but also amongst many converts who are jealous of you, because you have gained for yourself such a

European reputation, and got ahead of them. Your study, therefore, should be to stand well with the Holy See, and this you will do by showing yourself every year in Rome. Your being made Proto-Notary Apostolic will always give you an excuse, and at the same time increase your influence in the Curiâ.'[1]

With regard to the temporal power of the Pope, Manning completely changed his views in later life, as we shall presently see.

It must have been an awkward matter for Talbot to have to explain away Manning's prophecy that Rome would eventually become pagan, and would be the seat of Antichrist. By some the Popes had for years been stigmatized as Antichrists. Rome had originally retained numberless pagan customs, and had gradually introduced others, till at the present day, little is required but the change of name to render Rome again pagan.

We quote from 'Pagan and Popish Priestcraft identified and exposed,' by Rev. R. Taylor:

'Heathen priestcraft made void the Divine Law as epitomized in the Decalogue; philosophy, falsely so called, insinuated itself into the Church of Christ, and displaced the Christian precepts. And what has been called the "Christian Father" era of the third century caressed its seducing form in that spirit of conciliation which led the way to all the great truths being finally

[1] Vol. ii., p.'155.

amalgamated with the false notions of heathenism. The old heathen idolatry crept on serpent-like in a vain love of splendid buildings and glittering ornaments, till men believed there was a divinity in these; St. Cyril, a greater authority with some of our Tractarians than St. Paul, abused the sacraments, teaching that the flesh is renewed in this present life, instead of the vile body remaining vile till the general resurrection : then bringing in the worship of relics, prayers to and for the dead, saint worship in place of worshipping the old Pagan deities, and all Satan's other counterfeits of the Christian Church, with all their abominations, till finally the great Papal idol, the transubstantiated wafer, was erected, and Popery stood forth in all the fascinating, seducing pageantry and soul-destroying sensuality of the Eastern Baalim, and the dreadful potency of cruelty and terror of the Western Druidism.'

Manning, it must be remembered, in his Charge of July, 1841 (already quoted), had described the Church of Rome 'as inducing to sensual infidelity, and destitute of Christianity.'[1]

Pope, in the ' Dunciad,' well describes the mutations effected by Rome :

> ' See Peter's keys some christened Jove adorn,
>   And Pan to Moses lends his Pagan horn ;
> See graceless Venus to a virgin turned,
>   Or Phidias broken and Apelles burned.'

---

[1] Vol. i., p. 209.

In the *Churchman* for November, 1895, is a remarkable article by Canon Jenkins on the 'Bullarium Magnum,' in which he quotes the Jesuit von Hammerstein, who in his 'De Ecclesiâ et Statu,' pp. 112, 204 (1886), commenting on the encyclical 'Immortale Dei,' says that death by the flames is the only punishment effectual for the extirpation of heresy, and laments that the power of illustrating it practically has ceased.

In the *Revue Internationale de Théologie* for July to September, 1895, is an extract from an article in *Analecta Ecclesiastica* (a review approved and blessed by the Pope), by Father Pius de Langronio, which appeared in April, 1895, where he glorifies the work of the Inquisition and the horrible funeral-piles of Torquemada. 'Oh blessed flames of the funeral-piles! Oh glorious and venerable name of Thomas Torquemada!' The review continues: 'It is at Rome itself, and under the eyes of the pacific Leo XIII., that these barbarous and antichristian doctrines are printed.' *Cardinals Manning, Newman, and Vaughan would not answer Canon Jenkins as to whether these decrees against heretics are still in force.*

In our own Church at the present time, considerable discussion is being raised as to the best means of increasing the incomes of the poorer clergy. And yet how much is spent on the interior decorations of the churches, on vestments, etc. ! In a well-known church seven lamps have been recently presented, and these lamps have been endowed with a sufficient sum to produce an annual income of £25 for the purchase of oil, so that these lamps shall never be extinguished.

What deplorable ignorance at the close of the nineteenth century! Whence comes this practice of perpetual lights? From the pagan fire-worshippers. Is 'I am the Light of the World' (John viii. 12) totally forgotten?

In September, 1861, Manning wrote to Talbot:

'The only hope I see is in a coolness between France and England, which the bullying of Lord Palmerston and the newspapers has already in part produced. But English public opinion is blind, deaf, and unanimous against us.'[1]

Of what value were the statements made at the time of the passing of the Roman Catholic Disabilities Relief Bill, only a few years before?

Manning was ready to sacrifice his country, his patriotism, and for what? Not for the 'greater glory of God' or 'the salvation of souls,' but for the 'exaltation of the Church' and of himself. We do not believe that the 'poorest Catholic,' in England, at least, would express such sentiments. It is only the priests, and principally those in high places, who are so infected with the false principles of their precious

[1] Vol. ii., p. 167.

saint, Alphonso de Liguori, that they are unable to distinguish right from wrong, honour from dishonour, truth from falsehood.

Manning writes from Rome, on December 13, 1861, to Cardinal Wiseman:

'He [Cardinal Barnabò] said that Dr. Ullathorne had spoken to him on the subject of the restoration of Dr. Errington. Cardinal Barnabò answered that he had never thought him fit for Westminster and had always opposed the appointment. Dr. Ullathorne said he did not speak of his restoration to Westminster, but to some other see in England. . . . Now, it appears to me that your Eminence ought to know these facts. It appears to me that at some future day Dr. Errington's return to the Episcopate would be a question very different from what it is now. At this moment it would appear to be a reversal of the Holy Father's judgment in everything but form. It would seem to be a reaction of the Bishops against your last visit here and against yourself. It would give an impulse both in England and in the Episcopate to that which you have endeavoured to temper or to withstand. It would seem to convey the approval of the Holy See upon a course of administration which, if I know anything of England, would hinder the work of the Church both in itself and upon the English people more than anything but scandals, and, if I know anything of Rome, would not be what they desire or intend. But your Eminence sees all this far better than I do. As to Dr. Errington, I wish to see him treated with all respect due to a man who is personally good and upright; and if, hereafter, where no danger would result, he were replaced in some position, I should see it with satisfaction. But at this time, when the whole conflict is still under arms, and everything gained still precarious and at stake, and your work not consolidated, and in many ways already affected by reaction, and the old party not only biding their time, but exulting in the hope of change, and in their supposed gains in the diocese, and the Bishops sending a " procura " to Rome avowedly against your Eminence, I should look on any replacing of Dr. Errington, not as the restoration of a person, but as the reversal of a whole line of action, and the consolidation of its opposite.'[1]

In this letter we see Manning in his element. He is stirring up Cardinal Wiseman, and actively intriguing in Rome, against any appointment in England being offered to Dr. Errington, whom he (Manning) had ousted from his suffraganship and from the right of succession to the Metropolitical See of Westminster. The 'I wish to see him treated with all respect due to a man who is personally good and upright' is a piece of hypocritical cant that is worthy of such an intriguer. Dr. Errington's appointment to any bishopric in England might mean, should anything

[1] Vol. ii., p. 107.

happen to Cardinal Wiseman, his election as the Cardinal's successor, and this would, naturally, have been a death-blow to Manning's ambitions.

Three days later, on December 16, he again writes:

'On the subject of Dr. Errington it will be best not to take any step till I can write to you again. I have fully informed Monsignor Talbot, and I have had a long conversation with Dr. Ullathorne. I find he had no idea or desire to promote any steps on the subject; nor has any thought of Dr. Errington's restoration at this or any time, except a distant one. He spoke on the subject because some of the Bishops had desired it, and did not intend Cardinal Barnabò to take the matter up so practically, and will, I think, take care to counteract what he has done. I think, therefore, it will be best to let him act without any expression from you; but I would ask you to write, if you approve it, a letter addressed to Cardinal Barnabò, but to send it to me, to be used if there should be need, and to give me permission to communicate a copy of it to the Holy Father.'[1]

And on December 21, 1861:

'. . . Now, then, is the time I have often spoken of and long wished for. I will do my best, and write as full a review and estimate as I can of the whole contest of the last ten years. I have watched them

[1] Vol. ii., p. 108.

as closely as I could, and through your kindness I have been so mixed with them that I think I can judge of them, and I have been so irresponsible that I believe I can judge them impartially.'[1]

No doubt he could judge them, but we should doubt the 'impartiality.' How fared Canon Searle, Bishop Grant, and Dr. Errington under this judgment? We have seen in Manning's letters what he thought of all three, and we can only regret that the judgment is not before us. What would not a Diary of this period, with full detail of conversations and plots, have revealed?

The plot was successful, the impartial judgment had had its due effect, and Dr. Errington's promotion in the Church in England was effectually barred.

Manning returned to London, and Talbot wrote to him on July 18, 1862:

'There is no doubt that we enabled Cardinal Wiseman to gain a great triumph in Rome; but I hope he will make a proper use of it. I hope he will not boast of it, so that what he says should get to the ears of the other Bishops. I shall never forget their look after their last audience, in which the Pope gave them a severe lesson. Dr. Ullathorne was very bitter after it, and so was Grant. They both received a solemn rebuke to meditate on.'[2]

Why should Dr. Ullathorne be so 'very bitter,' if,

[1] Vol. ii., p. 144.   [2] Vol. ii., p. 110.

as Manning told Wiseman in his letter of December 16, 1861, he had only 'spoken because some of the Bishops had desired it, and did not intend Cardinal Barnabò to take up the matter so practically, and will, I think, take care to counteract what he has done'?

Had Manning deceived Wiseman in this matter by misrepresenting the conversation he had had with Dr. Ullathorne? Was his purpose to prevent Wiseman writing direct, get a request through Talbot to draw up a statement of the whole case himself, and so impress both the Pope and Cardinal Wiseman with his great zeal and energy for 'the greater glory of God, the exaltation of the Church, and the salvation of souls'?

Manning had written to Talbot on July 1, 1862:

'I will, as I have already, say all I can to the Cardinal; but I find him more open-hearted and amenable when he is in trouble, than when he is in prosperity, and this success will be a danger.'[1]

A most naïve admission. Who, then, was it that troubled the Cardinal during his illness—Manning or Searle?

Manning again wrote on August 16, 1862:

'The Cardinal will tell you of certain little busynesses (*sic*) of his which vex the Cardinal out of proportion; but they are very inconsiderate of Grant, and

[1] Vol. ii., p. 148.

his doings with the Government are more than that. Still, I have advised the Cardinal not to write formally to Rome about them, for he who throws the first stone will damage himself.'[1]

A 'note' explains this:

'Cardinal Wiseman, knowing that he was a *persona grata*, had deputed Manning to act on his behalf; but the Bishops, objecting to be represented by Manning, deputed Dr. Grant, the Bishop of Southwark, to act in their name, in transacting official business with the Government.'

We have now to trace a very pretty little intrigue on the part of the two allies to obtain the coadjutorship for Manning.

The latter wrote to Talbot on May 25, 1863:

'Cardinal Barnabò spoke very strongly on the dangers ahead to the diocese, to England, and to the Holy See in the event of the Cardinal's life and the Holy Father's failing. He desired me to repeat all this to the Cardinal. . . . I told the Cardinal the first part; the latter (of a new coadjutor) I have not yet said. It is a difficult subject for me to speak of, but I will endeavour to do so. I believe the Cardinal is still unwilling to look the question in the face; but it ought to be done.'[2]

To this Talbot replied on June 6, 1863:

'This brings me to the subject of Dr. Errington,

[1] Vol. ii., p. 150.   [2] Vol. ii., p. 173.

with whom nearly all of them seem to sympathize. I am afraid that Cardinal Bò's apprehensions are too well founded, and in the event of the Cardinal's death, I fear they will manifest the English national feeling working within them, and try to put him (Dr. Errington) at their head, in order to oppose the wishes of the Holy See. This scandal must be prevented. Cardinal Bò says, every time I see him, that the Cardinal must name a coadjutor.'[1]

And again on June 13, 1863:

'I am delighted to hear that Cardinal Wiseman has made up his mind to do what Cardinal Bò advises. But it is a most delicate matter, and requires the greatest secrecy, because, if it were to get abroad, there would be a great row among the Bishops. Cardinal Bò advised, and I am of the same opinion, that Cardinal Wiseman ought to write a letter to the Pope himself, couched in the kindest terms, and begging as a favour that he would generously grant him a coadjutor. It will be better also that he should name the person he wishes, as it will never do to allow the Chapter to send a *terna*. It is also important that Cardinal Bò should not be consulted, because he is so timid, and so much afraid of the English Bishops, that he would be afraid of a really fit man being chosen. All the Pope's past acts he has been opposed to, before they took place. I feel convinced that if

[1] Vol. ii., p. 173.

the Cardinal writes a letter such as he is so capable of doing, he will carry his point, and prevent a great scandal in England at his death. I feel convinced that all the Bishops in England would write to recommend Dr. Errington for Westminster, not from liking the man, but from an English feeling of triumph over Cardinal Wiseman, and gaining a victory over the Holy See. Perhaps Dr. Ullathorne might not join from private motives, and perhaps Dr. Cornthwaite from real goodness; but all the rest have not sufficient veneration for the Holy See so as to bow to its decrees and not act against their spirit.'[1]

We can quite understand Manning's difficulty in speaking to Cardinal Wiseman on the question of the coadjutorship, as any name, except that of Manning himself, would have met with the 'impartial judgment,' and that, as we shall see later (when Manning himself was a candidate for the archbishopric of Westminster) would not tend to the benefit of the candidate proposed.

We can understand, too, the sympathy felt for Dr. Errington. If others looked upon him as 'personally good and upright,' no wonder they considered he had been very hardly treated.

Mr. Purcell tells us that 'Cardinal Wiseman knew only too well were he to appoint Manning there would be such a hubbub as to destroy all chance of living or dying in peace.'[2]

---

[1] Vol. ii., p. 174. [2] Vol. ii., p. 180, note.

What was the Cardinal to do? He was not to be left in peace, then, at all events.

Cardinal Barnabò, the Provost of Propaganda, 'opposing all the acts of the Pope before they take place' is another glorious illustration of the boasted 'Unity' of the Roman Catholic Church, and of the estimate in which the infallible 'Vicar of Christ' is held by the higher orders in Rome. It is also an infallible commentary on Manning's letter to Robert Wilberforce of July 11, 1852:

'I have no words to express what is the Divine life and Divine reality of the Church in its acts.'

Manning wrote to Talbot on June 12, 1863:

'The Cardinal will write to you. He would be relieved if the Holy See would decide for him. He is timid, and wishes to end his days without any more troubles. But this is the way to greater troubles when he is gone. I feel restrained from speaking to him on the subject, but I can see that he would be very glad that the Holy Father should act. . . . But some who are near the Cardinal, I suspect, intimidate him. And Searle is Searle.'[1]

There was to be no peace for Cardinal Wiseman. Had the Holy Father acted, no doubt the effect of the 'whispers' would have been seen, and perhaps there would have been another '*coup d'état* of the Lord God,' as the Pope blasphemously phrases it.

[1] Vol. ii., p. 175.

CHAPTER XI.

TALBOT, in a letter to Manning under date October 10, 1863, says:

'I have just received your distressing letter about the Cardinal's health. Of course, I mentioned what you said about him to the Holy Father, and he was much grieved. Cardinal Barnabò, you know, takes such matters very lightly, but even he fears the consequence of his death.'[1]

Is callousness to be added to the other qualities of the followers of St. Alphonso de Liguori?

Is it all *meum et tuum*—Power and Influence?

Manning wrote on October 17, 1863:

'What you say of Dr. Errington is, I believe, certain. F. Barge the other day told me that he had heard, I believe, from the persons in whose presence Dr. Errington had said that the right of succession remained in him, and that on the Cardinal's death he should enter as a matter of course. If King Stork

[1] Vol. ii., p. 177.

comes the frogs must look sharp. I should regard such an event as a disaster for the diocese, and for the mission of the Church in England.'[1]

Also, on the same day:

'There is no one about him [Wiseman] to whom he can speak. Searle is worse than nobody, and is a burden and a trial. The Cardinal has an old affection for him, and Searle has become identified with his *material* affairs, so that the Cardinal cannot bear to remove or deprive him; but his illness, strangeness, and contrariety of mind make him a constant wear. Also he comes between the Cardinal and those in whom he finds what he needs. . . . There is a great deal more I will say, please God, when we meet.'[2]

Talbot wrote again in November, 1863, pressing that the letter should be sent to the Pope, and stating:

'I believe, if he was to write such a letter, as he knows, to the Holy Father himself, with *reservata* over it, so that it may not go to Propaganda, and send it through the Nuncio at Paris, that he would get named as his coadjutor *whom he chooses*. He stands well with the Pope.'[3]

The allies met in Rome before the close of the year, but what further revelations Manning made to Talbot does not appear.

---

[1] Vol. ii., p. 142.   [2] Vol. ii., p. 177.
[3] Vol. ii., p. 180.

Manning wrote to Wiseman on December 4, 1863:

'Cardinal Barnabò has twice spoken to me on a matter which he desired me to communicate to you. It is that on which Talbot has already written, as I understand. Cardinal Barnabò said that he had wished that some provision had been made three years ago, simultaneously with the decree respecting the *jus successionis*, so as to preclude, not only all risk of future complications, but the suspicions of party feelings which have been kept alive. This not having been done, he feels all the more strongly now, and that because of the refusal of Trinidad, the terms of the refusal, and the state of feeling which exists both in England and Ireland. Added to this the anxieties from time to time about yourself. On all this he said much that your Eminence will understand. I trust and believe that we shall have you many years among and over us; and I always feel that it does not shorten our life to make our will. Nevertheless, what Cardinal Barnabò said has been my strong and settled conviction, which, but for a certain delicacy, I should have more strongly expressed. I feel that I may and ought to do so now. After what he said, it seems to me that, if the Bishop referred to were invested with the right of succession, and *at once*, many great benefits would follow. It would put an end to all doubts, and all the *seditions* which spring from these doubts, and there are many, and near home. Also it would extinguish many *suspicions* which are very mischievous and very painful and very injurious to those whom they affect. It would also tranquillize the Bishops. This I said to Cardinal Barnabò, adding that the Bishop named is acknowledged by all, including his colleagues, to be the best and ablest.'[1]

Cardinal Wiseman's hand is to be forced somehow. The 'refusal of Trinidad,' above referred to, was the refusal by Dr. Errington of the archbishopric of Port of Spain, Trinidad. He did not wish to be banished from England and from Europe.

The 'suspicions' and 'seditions' among the higher ranks of the clergy do not lead us to conclude that the spiritual state of the infallible Church was such that the greater glory of God and the salvation of souls were its first objects. 'Unity,' of course, in such case is out of the question.

Mr. Purcell's comment on this letter is:

'Knowing only too well with what feelings Cardinal Wiseman regarded Dr. Ullathorne, the Bishop of Birmingham, first, as the head of the opposing Bishops, and, secondly, as the staunch supporter of Dr. Errington, whose removal he had bitterly resented, Manning, with his usual tact and delicacy, had carefully avoided in his first letter mentioning him by name as Wiseman's successor. But in his second

[1] Vol. ii., p. 181.

letter the obnoxious name was indicated by its initial.'[1]

We do not quite see Manning's 'delicacy' in this matter, but the 'tact' is perfectly apparent. To force Wiseman to name a coadjutor and successor, and to put forward before Propaganda the one man whom Wiseman would oppose with all the power and influence at his command (and Wiseman, to quote Talbot, 'stood well with the Pope'), was a display of 'tact' worthy of the best traditions of Roman intrigue.

The second letter referred to was written from Rome on December 8, 1863:

'I had yesterday an audience of three-quarters of an hour. Dr. U. was spoken of. I said that I heard you say the last time I saw you that the Holy Father could conclude the matter by a stroke of his pen; and I was sure that any wish or judgment formed by the Holy Father would have your entire assent. . . . I hope I have not gone against your wish in saying everything to Cardinal Barnabò and to the Holy Father in support of the appointment of Dr. U. I could do so with all my heart, for I have a very high sense of his goodness, both as a man and a Bishop; and I think him beyond all compare the fittest man to come after you.'[2]

Of course, what Manning said to Cardinal Barnabò and to the Pope, at his interview with him, may not

[1] Vol. ii., p. 182.   [2] Vol. ii., p. 182.

have been of the same tenor as the 'whispers' that reached the Pope's ears through Talbot. More light will be thrown on this inner working after Cardinal Wiseman's death.

Of course, the allies were perfectly aware that neither the Pope nor Propaganda would appoint a coadjutor to Wiseman without first obtaining, under Wiseman's own hand, his consent to the name of the person to be appointed.

In an autobiographical note, written December 23, 1882, Manning says: 'He [Wiseman] was much displeased, and when I came home said: "I felt as if my last friend had left me."'[1]

Manning returns to the charge, in a letter to Wiseman, on December 31, 1863:

'I feel certain that this is one of the *causæ majores* in which the Holy See is especially guided, and our Lord is especially present; so that after writing straight to the Holy Father, or, what is far better, speaking *facie ad faciem*, I feel you may rest in perfect peace.'[2]

After all that has gone before, after the letters from which we have given extracts, can it be called anything less than blasphemy to speak of 'our Lord being especially present'?

Wiseman was now to be forced to Rome if possible. That would have best suited the ends of the allies.

[1] Vol. ii., p. 183.   [2] Vol. ii., p. 184.

Had the Pope, primed by Talbot, asked Wiseman
'Why do you not appoint Manning?' what could have
been Wiseman's answer?

Manning added another last nail in a letter to
Wiseman, of February 1, 1864.

'Cardinal Barnabò told me last week that the
Chapter of Westminster had written to him asking
why they had not been consulted about the supposed
coadjutor. He was much excited about it, called it
una impertinenza. . . . Did your Eminence know this
fact? I told your Eminence, I believe, that Cardinal
Barnabò declared he had *never written to Dr. Ullathorne* on the subject you wrote about. What can be
the bottom of this?'[1]

Talbot had said in his letter (already quoted) of
June 13, 1863, that it 'was a most delicate matter and
required the greatest secrecy, because, if it were to
get abroad, there would be a great row among the
Bishops.' Cardinal Barnabò had denied having
written about it. The Pope's writing about it was out
of the question. 'What can be the bottom of this?'
Was this another instance of 'tact'? The intelligence
must have emanated from one of the two allies. Was
this all part of the scheme to force the Cardinal's
hand?

Cardinal Wiseman was not to be drawn. He not
only wrote a letter of remonstrance to Propaganda,

[1] Vol. ii., p. 187.

but also prohibited Manning from any further interference in the matter, as the following letter, addressed to him by Manning, and written from Rome on February 26, 1864, sufficiently shows:

'On the subject of the coadjutor, you may consider the matter as in your hands. Cardinal Barnabò read to me your letter, and said that the Holy Father had no intention of pressing anything, and that he should answer, leaving it to you. Also the Holy Father said the other day that he expected your Eminence in Rome, and that it would then be easier to consider the matter. . . . Since I had your letter of injunction I have been silent.'[1]

The suggestion is again made that Cardinal Wiseman should visit Rome, and that then the question could be finally settled; and this time the invitation is represented as coming from the Pope himself, but the state of Cardinal Wiseman's health prevented that visit from ever being paid.

Cardinal Wiseman died on February 15, 1865. Manning, in an autobiographical note, written in 1879, said: 'I got home on the morning of February 15, the very day on which he died.'[2] And yet he wrote to Lady Herbert, from Bayswater, on February 16, 1865: 'The Cardinal recalled me by telegraph to England; after sixty-eight hours, day and night, I came in time to watch by him for three days and three nights.'[3]

[1] Vol. ii., p. 188.   [2] Vol. ii., p. 192.   [3] Vol. ii., p. 240.

While in Rome Manning had constant information as to the state of the Cardinal, and on learning that there was no hope, he wished to return to England at once; but this the Pope prevented, as he believed Manning would only arrive too late. Having at last obtained permission, he arrived in London on the morning of February 13. We may excuse the mistake in the autobiographical note written fourteen years afterwards, but there can be no possible excuse for the deliberate false statement to Lady Herbert written the day after the Cardinal's death. There was no occasion to deceive Lady Herbert as to a matter of fact, unless it were for the exaltation of her father confessor and spiritual director.

He wrote to Talbot on February 13, 1865:

'Do not let Propaganda alarm itself; the majority of the laymen are sound. All they want is to be firmly led and told what to do. To hesitate or to be timid would be fatal. . . . Do not let Dr. Clifford again frighten them. I am told that the Thynnes and the like have been about him.'[1]

[1] Vol. ii., p. 192.

CHAPTER XII.

WE now enter on a new phase of the intrigue. It is no longer any question of a coadjutorship, successorship, or of a simple bishopric, but of the archbishopric itself. The persons named in the last-quoted letter were representatives of the old English Roman Catholic families, who strongly objected to a pushing and intriguing convert being placed at the head of the Church of Rome in England.

The Chapter of Westminster had the privilege of submitting a *terna*—that is, a list of three names—to Rome for the vacant appointment, and Manning writes to Talbot on February 24, 1865:

'... They may put Dr. Errington in the *terna*, but I do not expect it, because it would be too direct an opposition to the Holy See. I do not think they will put in Dr. Ullathorne, for he is not popular. My belief is they will put in Dr. Clifford, Dr. Grant, and perhaps Dr. Newman, for Oakeley and Dr. Maguire have been literally playing the fool about him in this Kingsley affair. I cannot for a moment even fear that the Holy See would accept any one of these names. I have chosen the three whom I believe in the sight of God to be the most attached to Rome, and to have the most love of souls. . . . Indeed, I hardly deprecate any appointment, except Dr. Errington and Dr. Clifford—and the latter even more than the former. We should be overrun with worldly Catholics and a worldly policy without his meaning or knowing it. One thing I feel, that is, how disastrous an arrangement it is that the choice of the Archbishop and Metropolitan, affecting therefore not Westminster only, but all England, should be even remotely affected by Maguire, Searle, O'Neal, Oakeley, Weathers, and Last. These six can outvote everyone. I wish the Holy Father would reserve the archbishopric in perpetuity to the Holy See. And I know no six men less acquainted with Rome or England or the needs of the Church in England. They are busy together and mean mischief. But God will take care of us. And this makes me very quiet and without fear.'[1]

Manning here says he does not expect Dr. Ullathorne's name to be included in the *terna*, because 'he is not popular,' and yet less than three months before he wrote to Cardinal Wiseman that he had told

[1] Vol. ii., p. 205.

Cardinal Barnabò that Dr. Ullathorne 'was acknowledged by all, including his colleagues, to be the best and ablest.

Again, Manning here says : 'I have chosen the three whom I believe in the sight of God to be the most attached to Rome, and to have the most love of souls.' But on the previous December 8 he had written to Cardinal Wiseman : 'I think him [Dr. Ullathorne] beyond all compare the fittest man to come after you.'

Had Dr. Ullathorne less attachment to Rome, or had he less love of souls, than he possessed three months before?

By this letter we must estimate the truth of his statement to Cardinal Barnabò, and of his letters to Cardinal Wiseman. St. Alphonso's doctrines would surely be inapplicable when dealing with such exalted officials of the Church of Rome.

We see in this letter in what estimation Manning held Dr. Clifford, though he was the first on the list of those 'whom I believe in the sight of God to be the most attached to Rome, and to have the most love of souls.' Was Dr. Clifford likely to show himself more worldly than Manning has depicted himself in these letters?

As to Dr. Grant, the second on the list, we must not forget the story of 'the . . . and the smoking and drinking,' as told to Talbot in the letter of

August 17, 1860, ending with, 'The Cardinal is detested by the boys, and Dr. Grant in great repute; this is the work of Dr. Grant and his Southwark friends.' Nor must we forget that Dr. Grant had received from the Pope a 'solemn rebuke to meditate on,' as Talbot told Manning in the letter of July 18, 1862.

As to Dr. Newman, the third name in the list, Mr. Purcell explains the allusion to 'Oakeley and Dr. Maguire literally playing the fool about him' in a note:

'Father Newman's "Apologia pro Vitâ suâ," in which he demolished Kingsley's calumnious charge of teaching as a priest that "truth is not a virtue." [1]

Whether Newman taught it as a priest or not, there were other priests who acted on that teaching.

Manning's own relations to, and opinions of, Newman we shall see later.

There is a strong indictment in this letter against six members of the Chapter of Westminster, to some of whom we shall refer later.

No doubt the Pope's taking the matter into his own hands would have perfectly suited the allies. The 'coup d'état of the Lord God' had already once been in Manning's favour, and there was no reason to doubt that he would not profit by the exercise of it again.

[1] Vol. ii., p. 205, note.

Mr. Purcell informs us that between the date of this last letter, 'February 24, and March 18, 1865, there is a break in the correspondence between Dr. Manning and Monsignor Talbot. Either no letters were interchanged during those weeks of suspense and speculation, or the correspondence has not been preserved.'[1]

We should incline to the latter hypothesis, looking to the fact of the numerous letters that passed between them on every occasion on which a *coup* was to be effected either in Rome or in London, and this was the greatest occasion that occurred in their joint lives.

In the first subsequent letter, on March 18, 1865, Talbot tells Manning :

'Dr. Clifford has been writing to Rome, recommending Errington. This must be told to the Pope. He, of course, knew all the circumstances of Errington's removal, yet nevertheless he has the audacity to recommend him. Capital ought to be made out of this fact.'[2]

Manning was suggested to Cardinal Barnabò by Talbot as a candidate for the vacant archbishopric, but was strongly opposed by the Cardinal.

Talbot thereupon wrote a letter to Canon Morris to break the news to Manning, and the latter's reply on March 31, 1865, is characteristic :

[1] Vol. ii., p. 207, note.   [2] Vol. ii., p. 207.

'Canon Morris sent me your letter; and I thank you sincerely for your kind thought about me. If I were to say that the object of it had not been before my mind, I should go beyond the truth; for in the last years, both in England and abroad, people have, out of kind but inconsiderate talk, introduced the subject. But if I say that I never for a moment believed the thing to be probable, reasonable, or imaginable, I should speak the strict truth. I have therefore never, as you once said people thought, "aimed at it" or desired it. God knows I have never so much as breathed a wish to Him about it. And in all this time I have been as indifferent as if nothing were pending. I believe I may say that God knows I have lived for work and not names or promotions. If I had refused what the Holy Father has hitherto given me, men would have believed this without my saying it; but if I had refused it, I doubt if I should have done the will of God. . . . And I know that nothing can take off the edge of the truth, and that, under God, is all I have ever trusted to, long before I was a Catholic. Be sure I look for nothing; and be sure, too, that as long as I have life and strength you will find me going straight on in the same road, in which I have always felt you have gone yourself without fear.'[1]

A most admirable letter for Talbot to show to the

[1] Vol. ii., p. 209.

Pope, as no doubt it was shown, or at least read, to him.

In his Anglican life Manning told us he 'never asked for' anything, and never 'canvassed.' Now he does not 'aim at it.' Blackening the character of every possible candidate does not show him 'as indifferent as if nothing were pending.'

What can we think of all the intrigues and the attempts to force Cardinal Wiseman's hand in the matter of the coadjutorship? Can we forget Manning's proposing Dr. Ullathorne for the post, knowing full well that he would be strongly opposed, not only by Cardinal Wiseman, but by the Bishops as well?

'I have lived for work, and not names or promotions.' Newman might more properly have said this. He had now been in the Church of Rome for twenty years, and was still Father Newman, of the Oratory at Birmingham. But those who have followed Manning's career so far will see with what justice Manning could apply the above sentence to himself.

If 'truth is all he ever trusted to, long before he was a Catholic,' we must ask again, with Pilate, What is truth? It cannot be the 'straight road' of St. Alphonso's doctrines, deceit, falseness, ambition, and intrigue.

Talbot kept Manning well informed of what was going on, and wrote on March 28, 1865:

'It appears that Lord Palmerston, through Odo

Russell, has been recommending Clifford and Grant; and as Antonelli has no ecclesiastical spirit, never having worked as a priest, he takes the diplomatic view of trying to conciliate the English Government, by accepting one of the names proposed to him, and at the same time to sympathize with the worldly Catholics. It is the concordat of Portugal over again. He would have ruined the Church in India to please the Portuguese Government, and so now he thinks it more important to conciliate the English Government and Lord Palmerston, than to convert and sanctify souls. Now, the great point of anxiety with me is whether a congregation will be held, or whether the Holy Father will perform a Pontifical act. He himself is doubting. I therefore say Mass and pray every morning that he may have the courage to choose for himself, instead of submitting the matter to a congregation.'[1]

It must be news to many Roman Catholics to be told that Cardinal Antonelli had 'no ecclesiastical spirit.' They, and others, can remember the estimation in which he was held during his life, and the high encomium passed on him at his death.

Had Talbot ever 'worked as a priest'? How came he, then, by this ecclesiastical spirit? What distinction is there between the diplomatic and the ecclesiastical spirit of Rome? Is it the ecclesiastical spirit that

[1] Vol. ii., p. 210.

impels them to continually invoke the name of their Creator in all their intrigues and ambitions?

Manning writes in reply to this on April 3, 1865:

'You have said truly this is another concordat with Portugal.

> '1. If the Government finds it is listened to, we shall have it meddling in England and in Ireland in the appointment of Bishops—meddling both for and against the men it can rule, or that it fears.
>
> '2. Also, we shall have priests making up to Government, and shaping their course so as to stand well for promotion.
>
> '3. This will be the worst of *vetoes*, and will bring a corrupt and worldly spirit into our clergy, and form two parties, a Roman and English, which is our danger already. If we are divided, we are ruined.

'If the man recommended by Lord Palmerston were in every way fit, I trust the Holy See would never listen. It seems to me that a high principle is violated by such an attempt. The Papal aggression saved us from this danger once God forbid that we should give away our independence now. You have saved British India from one concordat; save us from this. As to writing to Cardinal Bò, I feel an insurmountable reluctance. I have never written to him since I announced the Cardinal's death. What you said most justly of him in your letter to Morris makes me hesitate all the more; though I knew it before. He knows what I think, and that I look upon the whole *terna* as Dr. Errington in three, and that it is a struggle to gain the ascendency over the Cardinal's work and name, and to justify their past insubordination. It is a grave affront to the Holy See, and Rome is far more at stake than the diocese of Westminster.'[1]

Manning, in the second and third reasons given in this letter, must surely have been condemning himself. What had he throughout his life done but 'shape his course so as to stand well for promotion'? He had 'made up' to the authorities of the English Church; he had taken up Tractarianism when he saw it was 'becoming a power in the land'; he had dropped it when he saw it was 'losing ground'; he had never, 'early or late in life, been partial to a losing cause'; and when all this had been of no avail, he turned his attention to the ruling powers in the Church of Rome. He had 'made up' to the Pope, to Talbot, and to Wiseman; he had 'removed, with far-reaching foresight, obstacles from his path, and made sure the foundations of his future career.'[2]

All this must surely be taken as showing a 'corrupt and worldly spirit' in a very high degree.

We see in this letter the estimate the conspirators

[1] Vol. ii., p. 212.   [2] Vol. i., p. 273.

formed of Cardinal Barnabò. To whom, then, did they pin their faith? To the Pope alone, apparently: but even in his case Manning's opinion underwent considerable change in later years.

In the Diary of May, 1846, we were told, 'Our divisions [in the Church of England] seem to me to be fatal as a token and as a disease.'[1]

What is the judgment, then, on the divisions in the Church of Rome?

If Cardinal Barnabò knew what Manning really thought, he must have had an extraordinary ' insight into the invisible,' unless Manning meant that he (Manning) was the only possible candidate.

The latter part of the letter was eminently qualified to rouse the Pope to extreme measures, and to bring about another *coup d'état.*

Manning's next letter is rather startling. He supposes Talbot himself is to receive the vacant appointment, and writes on April 11, 1865:

'I trust you will be sent to us. . . . Do not let anyone alarm you or anyone else with notions of dissensions, and schism, and the like. It is all absurd. I would answer for the union and peace of the future, if only the Holy See acts for itself.'[2]

Talbot explains that he has more power and influence where he is—in other words, that it would be no promotion to him.

[1] Vol. i., p. 484.   [2] Vol. ii., p. 214.

This letter is another bid for a 'Pontifical act,' and shows that the higher orders of the Roman Catholic clergy in England were not so black as they were painted.

The allies were successful, and Manning received the appointment of Archbishop of Westminster, and Metropolitan of the Church of Rome in England, having been a member of that Church for exactly fourteen years.

CHAPTER XIII.

AFTER this important result of all their intrigues together, Talbot writes to Manning:

'*My* policy throughout was never to propose you *directly* to the Pope, but to make others do so; so that both you and I can always say that it was not I who induced the Holy Father to name you, which would lessen the weight of your appointment. This I say because many have said that your being named was all my doing. I do not say that the Pope did not know that I thought you the only man eligible, as I took care to tell him over and over again what was against all the other candidates; and, in consequence, he was almost driven into naming you. After he had named you the Holy Father said to me, "What a diplomatist you are to make what you wished come to pass!" Nevertheless, I believe your appointment was specially directed by the Holy Ghost. Every free Mass I offered up for you; but at the same time I told them all that I thought you had no chance, in order to silence them. And I did not tell them an untruth, as I did not think the Holy Father would have had the moral courage which it required to name you against so much opposition. I have many more things to tell you about this matter, but I shall wait till we meet."[1]

It is abominable blasphemy to drag in the name of the Holy Ghost into their miserable intrigues and subterfuges. But we have been already prepared for this special form of blasphemy. Talbot, as we anticipated, acknowledges here that he used, to the fullest extent, the depreciation of all possible candidates, details for which had been supplied him by Manning, and yet he can say the 'appointment was specially directed by the Holy Ghost.' We have here, too, a supereminent example of the result of St. Alphonso's teaching, indulged in, too, even after 'offering up Mass.'

We shall never hear the 'many more things' that were to be told, but the letters tell us enough to enable us to form an 'impartial judgment' of the whole matter.

Manning, on receipt of the news, wrote to Talbot on May 9, 1865:

'I had fully hoped that you would be sent to us; or if not you, I looked for Dr. Ullathorne. But God has willed otherwise. I hardly know what to write.

[1] Vol. ii., p. 220.

But before all I must express my sense of your uprightness. I know all you have wished and done; but I know that you have acted for no human kindness, but for the salvation of souls, and the service of the Church. Pray for me as I never fail in every Mass to do for you.'[1]

This was followed by another letter on May 12, 1865:

'I ascribe altogether what has passed, and is passing, to the same prayers and Masses which, as you say, have caused the Holy Father to elect me. . . . The Holy Father may well be anxious to know that his act has made no storm. There is none, and, except through my future fault, will not be.'[2]

Two letters undoubtedly written for the Pope's eye. Manning had not expected Talbot to be sent. The idea of Talbot being chosen was quite an afterthought on Manning's part, and was promptly contradicted by Talbot himself. Nor could Manning pretend that he had 'looked for Dr. Ullathorne,' after telling Talbot of his unpopularity, and when Talbot knew too that he was the head and front of the opposition to Cardinal Wiseman. Manning's description of the *terna* applied in a greater degree to Dr. Ullathorne.

Talbot was 'upright' when he was advancing Manning's interests, and so was the Pope. But

[1] Vol. ii., p. 221. [2] Vol. ii., p. 223.

when the latter opposed Manning, another term was used to describe his conduct. But we must not forestall.

Talbot had not said the 'prayers and Masses had caused the Holy Father to elect' Manning. What he did say was that he did not put Manning's name forward himself, but got others to do so, and that he 'took care to tell the Pope over and over again what was against all the other candidates, and, in consequence, he was almost driven to naming you.' He even acknowledged that if all he had done were known, it would 'lessen the weight of your appointment.'

Had the divining nun any part in this appointment, and had Talbot and Manning squared her?

If there was no 'storm' after what we must call almost a revolutionary proceeding on the part of the Pope, in appointing a comparatively new convert as the head of the Church of Rome in England, what becomes of the stories about all the Bishops, and about the six members of the Chapter of Westminster, related by Manning to Talbot?

We next have two letters of Manning's sent to penitents. They may be described as 'beautiful little sermons, but mean nothing.' They speak for themselves.

The first to Lady Herbert, written on May 20, 1865:

'My dear Child,

'This letter will, I hope, find you at Venice, to tell you that, if all prospers, the consecration will be on June 8. I hope you will be here by that time, for I know you will pray for me. If, indeed, it were the will of our Divine Lord to lay upon me this heavy burden, He could have done it in no way more strengthening or consoling to me. To receive it from the hands of His Vicar, and from Pius IX., and after long invocation of the Holy Ghost, and not only without human influences, but in spite of manifold and powerful human opposition, gives me the last strength for such a cross. It is as if I had heard our Lord call me. And in this I can forget my own self and my manifold unworthiness. It has also here put me and my unworthiness out of mind; and the Bishops, the Chapter, and the Diocese have received the Holy Father's will, and me in it, in a way which I cannot repeat. I am so pressed that I can write but little, yet in that little I must say what joy it is to me to count you one of my Flock, and one of the true Flock, and of the one Fold. Life is wonderful, and I feel as if I should wake up, and find I had been dreaming. Be sure that all I can ever do for your guidance, I will. When you return, I shall be at York Place; but I shall keep my little room here. It is a great wrench to leave this house. I will write to Cardinal Reisach. I know his affection and goodness towards me. God be with you, and with your children. Have great faith and great trust in the love of the Sacred Heart to them and to you, and in the prayers of our Blessed Mother.'[1]

The second letter is to a 'penitent,' written on June 1, 1865, from Manning's 'retreat' at Highgate:

'MY DEAR CHILD,

'I have in these three last weeks felt as if our Lord had called me by name. Everything else has passed out of my mind. The firm belief I have long had that the Holy Father is the most supernatural person I have ever seen has given me this feeling more deeply still. I feel as if I had been brought, contrary to all human wills, by the Divine Will, into an immediate relation to our Divine Lord. The effect on me is one of awe, not fear; but a conscious nearness to God, and to the supernatural agencies and sufferings of His Church. . . . I believe I can say that what has come upon me has not raised my pulse one beat, that it has given no joy or personal gratification. I have lived for work, and little else, and I look upon this as so much work. It has brought some sadness, for I must lose for ever much of the happiness of a pastor's life, and nearly all my peace and rest. If anything has consoled me, it is the feeling that, if the Vicar of our Lord trusts me,

[1] Vol. ii., p. 228.

our Lord does not distrust me. And, if he has not lifted me up for my greater reprobation, He has chosen me to do Him some service in the few years of my time, whether by life or by death.'[1]

Is there a word of truth in either of these letters? Could these penitents have followed the intrigue, as we have been enabled to do, what would they have thought on receiving such letters as these? Where was Manning's conscience that he could write 'not only without human influences'? How dare he speak about 'the invocation of the Holy Ghost' when Talbot had told him that he had practically forced the Pope to name him? The blasphemy of the second letter is even worse than that of the first.

We have not seen much of Manning's 'sufferings,' though he alluded to them in a letter to Cardinal Wiseman, but he was undoubtedly, through his intrigues, the cause of much suffering to others in the Church of Rome.

How can Manning speak of 'losing for ever much of the happiness of a pastor's life, and all his peace and rest'? He had said the same to Cardinal Wiseman so long ago as April 14, 1857, on his appointment to the provostship of the Chapter of Westminster. What was the concluding paragraph in his Diary, 1851-54?

[1] Vol. ii., p. 230.

'I am conscious of a desire to be in such a position
'(1) As I had in times past;
'(2) As my present circumstances imply by the act of others;
'(3) As my friends think me fit for;
'(4) As I feel my own faculties tend to.'[1]

What did he write to Robert Wilberforce on April 1, 1856?

'God knows what it has cost me to be a priest, and to do the work of a priest, and to bear the name of a priest here in the midst of kindred and old friends and the world in which I lived before.'[2]

Again, 'If the Vicar of our Lord trusts me, our Lord does not distrust me.'

Yet Mr. Purcell tells us:

'The Holy See had taken a wise, if a bold step. Pope Pius IX. even had misgivings—not as to Manning, but as to the circumstances of the nomination.'[3]

What! after all the prayers and Masses by this most 'supernatural person'; after 'long invocation of the Holy Ghost'; after Manning's sense of 'being called,' of an 'immediate relation to our Divine Lord,' of a 'conscious nearness to God'! The 'most supernatural person's' keen insight into the invisible world should have made his judgment infallible. It was afterwards pronounced so by the famous Council of

[1] Vol. ii., p. 17.   [2] Vol. ii., p. 46.   [3] Vol. ii., p. 254.

1870, which was mainly engineered by Manning. Yet the Pope had 'misgivings as to the circumstances of the nomination.'

What, then, becomes of 'the Divine life and the Divine reality of the Church in its acts'? Canon Hearn wrote to Manning on April 25, 1865:

'I hasten to congratulate you on the news just come from Rome. Long live the new Archbishop of Westminster! Now the memory of the poor dear Cardinal is honoured. Now the Holy Father has proved that he really loved and admired him. One thing augurs well for you: you are the appointed of the Holy Ghost. For the Pope has had prayers and Masses said beyond number, and has himself been in communion with God for days and days May our Lord bless and guide you!'[1]

Mr. Purcell's comment is:

'The tone and spirit of the letter must have been a surprise to Manning, if not a rebuke.'[2]

Manning had a letter of congratulation from the clergy of the diocese of Birmingham, and, in answering it, wrote to the Provost of Birmingham:

'. . . I feel also the delicacy of your kindness for the reason which, as you say, prompted you to express it. A certain class of persons, who watch the expansion of the Catholic Church with no goodwill, have

[1] Vol. ii., p. 244.   [2] Vol. ii., p. 244.

thought to find or to make divisions among us. No doubt they imagined to have the best of opportunities at this moment. But division among us they can neither find nor make, not even at such a time as this. And your act, wholly unlooked for, without any of the ordinary motives of personal friendship, or of ecclesiastical relations, or of services rendered by me, to call forth such an expression on your part, is an evidence of the union of heart and mind which, as no system but the Church of God can produce, so none who are out of it can understand.'[1]

Another letter worthy of St. Alphonso himself. Had there been no divisions among them, even without this 'best of opportunities'? If the 'union of heart and mind' was so complete, there was no need for this fulsome letter. It was a very ordinary act on the part of the clergy in addressing their Metropolitan. There may have been no 'personal friendship,' or 'ecclesiastical relations,' or 'services rendered' in the past; but the ecclesiastical relations then existed, and the services, perhaps, were to be rendered in the future.

Manning had a letter of congratulation written from Rio Janeiro, and dated June 6, 1865:

'... Poor Searle! I wrote a very kind letter to him on the death of the Cardinal; I think he must have been nearly broken-hearted—at least, he ought

[1] Vol. ii., p. 248.

to have been, reviewing all the past—and I wrote to him as such. I am sure you will be magnanimous to him and a hundred other poor devils who will think "you are come to torment them before the time." [1]

Cardinal Vaughan, the Father Vaughan of this letter, has been very bitter against Mr. Purcell for publishing this book, and at first expressed the opinion that Cardinal Manning never intended it to be published so soon after his death. On second thoughts Cardinal Vaughan stated his opinion in the *Nineteenth Century* for February, 1896, that 'during the last few years [of Manning's life] the process of senile decay had set in. . . . After eighty his nature began to give way and break.'

Into the latter question we need not enter. Mr. Sydney Buxton has done so effectually in the *Fortnightly Review* for March, 1896.

We are surprised by the idea of Roman Catholic priests being 'tormented.' We understood they passed their time of expiation in Purgatory. It is only we poor Protestants, with all other heretics, who are condemned to be 'tormented.'

The letter speaks well for that marvellous union 'which no system but the Church of God can produce.'

Manning wrote to Talbot on June 9, 1865:

'I have named Canon O'Neal Vicar-General, for

[1] Vol. ii., p. 245.

many reasons which you would, I know, approve. So long as I have health and strength, it matters little who is Vicar-General. If I were to fail I know what to do. This appointment has done its work in the diocese, and taken from the Chapter and the old clergy a possible grievance. Also, Canon O'Neal is good, and to me has shown himself most compliant.'[1]

In Talbot's answer of July 10, 1865, he says:

'. . . As for myself, during the whole of the last affair, I have been on good terms with him [Cardinal Barnabò]; and we only had one little spar when I told him, after the death of the Cardinal, that you were the man to succeed him. At that time he was strongly opposed to you; but he watched the mind of the Pope, and came round at last. . . . The real motive why the Pope named you is because he thought you were the man to introduce a new spirit into the Church in England, which required it, as was seen by the conduct of the Chapter and the Bishops. . . . One thing, however, is most wonderful—the change of the opinion of Catholics in your favour; your greatest enemies have entirely come round. I received the other day a panegyric of you from Searle. This change of feeling I cannot attribute to anything but the Holy Ghost.'[2]

Here, then, is another 'true reason' of the Pope's

[1] Vol. ii., p. 232.   [2] Vol. ii., p. 256.

naming Manning. There seem to be as many 'true reasons' as there are 'true relics.'

If a 'new spirit is required in the Church in England,' the old spirit must necessarily have been corrupt. Where, then, is the boasted 'Unity'? We can explain the 'changed feeling' without any need for blasphemously dragging in the name of the Holy Ghost.

Manning has told Talbot that he had appointed O'Neal Vicar-General 'for many reasons which you would, I know, approve.' Manning himself then gives the chief reason, that it 'had taken from the Chapter and the old clergy a possible grievance,' and added that it 'had done its work in the diocese.' O'Neal was, as we have seen, one of the six impeached members of the Chapter of Westminster.

Manning also gives a reason for the 'panegyric from Searle' in a note in his Journal, July 9, 1879:

'I remember I told Monsignor Searle to go on as œconomus, and to make up his income to £300. He said, "I have long been looking with anxiety to this day; but you have changed my anxiety to consolation."'[1]

Manning had thus cut away the ground from under his opponents' feet, and it is small wonder that there was therefore 'a change of feeling.' 'Poor Searle's' consolation was short lived.

[1] Vol. ii., p. 256.

As Mr. Purcell tells us :

'A few years later Archbishop Manning deprived Canon Searle of his office. In consequence of some error in management, the Archbishop wrote to Monsignor Searle, "You are no longer œconomus of mine." [1]

[1] Vol. ii., p. 256, note.

CHAPTER XIV.

THE three next letters must be very peculiar reading for Roman Catholics.

The first is from Talbot to Manning, dated November 11, 1865:

'. . . I dare say I shall have many opportunities to serve you in Rome, because I see many questions brooding in the distance which will require my aid, and I do not think my support will be useless to you, especially on account of the peculiar character of the Pope, and the spirit which pervades Propaganda, therefore I wish you to understand that a compact exists between us; if you help me, I shall help you, and make you stand well in Rome, which in your position will be of great importance to you, as you have more secret opponents in England than you think you have, and you will see this before very long.'[1]

The second letter is again from Talbot to Manning, dated December 1, 1865:

[1] Vol. ii., p. 264.

'I am glad you accept the league. As I have already done for years, I shall support you, and I have a hundred ways of doing so. A word dropped at the proper occasion works wonders. At present your chief enemy in Rome is Monsignor Nardi, but he has committed so many blunders that he has not much power.'[1]

The third letter is from the same to the same, dated December 26, 1865:

'... I think you left Rome with false impressions regarding the Holy Father and Merode. The Holy Father is a very good man, but, as I said to you, he is not a saint. He has his weaknesses, but in the Merode affair he was perfectly right.'[2]

Here is evidence of a written treaty between the two allies for mutual help. Hitherto, the benefits had all been on Manning's side, but now Manning was in a position to return the compliment by putting forward Talbot's friends.

How well Manning kept to the agreement is told by Mr. Purcell:

'Monsignor Talbot used to complain that, when no longer needing his help, Archbishop Manning neglected him.'[3]

We have had reflections passed on many of the dignitaries of the Roman Catholic Church, but now

---

[1] Vol. ii., p. 265.   [2] Vol. ii., p. 267.
[3] Vol. ii., p. 696, note.

we have the Pope himself attacked. He has a 'peculiar character,' and 'is not a saint.'

How can we reconcile the statement in the first of these letters, 'you have more secret opponents in England than you think you have, and you will see this before very long,' with that in the letter of July 10, 1865, 'your greatest enemies have entirely come round,' and 'the change of opinion of Catholics in your favour'? Were the congratulatory letters, and the repentance proved by them, after all, only 'beautiful little sermons which meant nothing'?

The unity of these Roman Catholics is 'wonderful'; they have such fervent charity that they can trust no one.

Manning at once made use of the compact.

'Within the first year of his episcopate, Manning wrote strongly urging the nomination of Dr. Chadwick to the vacant See of Hexham, describing the other two candidates named in the *terna* as unsuitable for various reasons for the episcopal office.'[1]

Talbot wrote in reply :

'You will be glad to learn that Dr. Chadwick has been appointed to the See of Hexham.'[2]

We now come to the discussion of the relations between Manning and Newman.

The former wrote to Talbot on February 25, 1866 :

[1] Vol. ii., p. 269.   [2] Vol. ii., p. 270.

'What you write about Dr. Newman is true. Whether he knows it or not, he has become the centre of those who hold low views about the Holy See, are anti-Roman, cold and silent, to say no more, about the temporal power, national, English, critical of Catholic devotions, and always on the lower side. . . . I see much danger of English Catholicism, of which Newman is the highest type. It is the old Anglican, patristic, literary, Oxford tone transplanted into the Church. It takes the line of deprecating exaggerations, foreign devotions, Ultramontanism, anti-national sympathies. In one word, it is worldly Catholicism, and it will have the worldly on its side, and will deceive many.'[1]

Talbot had written on February 20, 1866:

'. . . You will have battles to fight, because every Englishman is naturally anti-Roman. To be Roman is to an Englishman an effort. Dr. Newman is more English than the English. His spirit must be crushed.'[2]

Which could fairly be accused of worldly religion, Manning or Newman?

The one had been twenty years in the Church of Rome, and was still simply a priest at the Oratory at Birmingham; he had been mistrusted by friends and foes alike—had been even accused of being out of his mind; he had borne no share in the intrigues for

[1] Vol. ii., p. 322.   [2] Vol. ii., p. 322, note.

promotion, nor in the discussion of politico-ecclesiastical questions, nor had he been continually visiting Rome to keep himself *en évidence.* The course of the other we have traced.

Newman had been strongly attacked in all the Roman Catholic papers, but more especially in the *Dublin Review*, and Talbot had slightly remonstrated in a letter of April 19, 1866, to which Manning replied:

'You may rest satisfied that nothing is published which does not pass under the censure of three competent ecclesiastics, and I mostly see every critical article.'[1]

Mr. Purcell's comment on this is:

'For those aspersions then on Newman which did appear in the *Dublin Review*—and they were fierce and frequent—Archbishop Manning was responsible, since they were published under his tacit sanction. But of course the way in which Newman was attacked in conversation and correspondence was infinitely worse than what was published in the Archbishop's *Review*. On the very day of his consecration, when he had not only invited Newman to be present at the function, but had spoken of him, to Ward's horror, with sympathy, Archbishop Manning was once more warned in the following words of the dangers of conciliation: "Of course there is a very

[1] Vol. ii., p. 308.

dangerous extreme to be avoided. But is it not also dangerous to speak of John Henry Newman with *simple* sympathy? If it is true (and I for one have no doubt at all) that he is exercising a most powerful influence in favour of what is in fact (though he doesn't think so)—(1) Disloyalty to the Vicar of Christ, (2) Worldliness—is not harm done by conveying the impression that there is no cause for distrust?" [1]

This was a true exhibition of the principles of St. Alphonsus—to say one thing, and mean another; to speak with sympathy one day, and to allow such a statement to appear in his paper the next.

Manning wrote to Talbot on April 13, 1867:

'You will see in the *Tablet* an address to Dr. Newman, signed by most of our chief laymen. . . . Do not let Propaganda alarm itself. . . . It will be necessary to take care that no such letters from Rome be sent to our papers. Can you do anything?'[2]

---

[1] Vol. ii., p. 309.
[2] Vol. ii., p. 315. The attacks on Newman published by an anonymous Roman correspondent of a Catholic paper were, though different in form, identical in substance with the charges made in the correspondence between Monsignor Talbot and Manning. Monsignor Talbot was naturally anxious that his name should not be mentioned in connection with the newspaper affair. In reply Manning wrote that he had guarded against any such allusion (Vol. ii., p. 316, note).

What did 'Can you do anything?' mean? Had Talbot himself written those letters?

Talbot wrote on April 25, 1867 :

'Dr. Newman is the most dangerous man in England, and you will see that he will make use of the laity against your Grace. You must not be afraid of him. It will require much prudence, but you must be firm, as the Holy Father still places his confidence in you ; but if you yield and do not fight the battle of the Holy See against the detestable spirit growing up in England, he will begin to regret Cardinal Wiseman, who knew how to keep the laity in order. I tell you all this in confidence, because I already begin to hear some whisperings, which might become serious.'[1]

The latter part of the letter contains a veiled threat, but Manning hardly required this egging on. He saw how the land lay, and took his course accordingly.

Manning had written to Newman to try to put a false gloss over their future relations, and received the following reply, dated August 10, 1867 :

'. . . You are quite right in thinking that the feelings, of which, alas ! I cannot rid myself in my secret heart . . . have nothing to do with the circumstance that you may be taking a line in ecclesiastical matters which does not approve itself to my judgment. Certainly nôt ; but you must kindly bear with me, though

[1] Vol. ii., p. 317.

I seem rude to you, when I give you the real interpretation of it. I say frankly, then, and as a duty of friendship, that it is a distressing mistrust, which now for four years past I have been unable in prudence to dismiss from my mind, and which is but my own share of a general feeling (though men are slow to express it, especially to your immediate friends). I wish I could get myself to believe that the fault was my own, and that your words, your bearing, and your implications ought, though they have not served, to prepare me for your acts. No explanation offered by you at present in such a meeting [a meeting proposed by Archbishop Manning] could go to the root of the difficulty, as I have suggested it. . . . It is only as time goes on that new deeds can reverse the old. There is no short cut to a restoration of confidence, when confidence has been seriously damaged.'[1]

Then, Newman even in his retirement at his Oratory of Birmingham saw the difference between Manning's words, bearing, and implications, and his acts which should have followed on them but did not. But why only 'the last four years'? Should not Manning's whole career in his Anglican life have thoroughly prepared Newman for this last four years? Could Newman have forgotten Manning's dealings with himself and with the Tractarians—open and otherwise? Or was he so imbued with his false system of logic that

[1] Vol. ii., p. 305.

the deceit and hypocrisy which were pardonable in the Anglican Church were sufficient to cause a want of confidence when carried out in the Roman Catholic Church? Manning answered this letter on August 14, 1867:

'I have felt in you exactly what you felt in me, and that feeling I share also, as you say, with others. I cannot put my meaning into more precise and delicate words than by using your own. I have felt you difficult to understand, and that your words have not prepared me for your acts. This I know to be a feeling respecting you, as you find it respecting myself. Now, I feel with you that the root of the difficulty is a mutual mistrust; and, as you say, this is hard to cure.'[1]

In what way had Newman's acts belied his words since he had joined the Church of Rome?

It is true that in his 'Apologia pro Vitâ suâ' he had boasted that he was an Englishman, and, further, that he 'would rather be an Englishman than belong to any other race under heaven' (Preface, xvi).

We have seen what the other side of the question is in Manning's letter to Talbot of September, 1861:

'The only hope I see is in a coolness between France and England.'[2]

The pro-Roman would prefer the temporal power of his Church to the welfare of his country. Christ

[1] Vol. ii., p. 306.   [2] Vol. ii., p. 167.

Himself said, 'My kingdom is not of this world, else would My servants fight;' but the infallible Vicar of Christ says, ' My kingdom *is* of this world, and my servants *shall* fight for it.'

Manning wrote to Talbot on September 14, 1867:

'I have made an attempt to soften Dr. Newman, but he is very difficult. We ended by a promise to say Masses for each other.'[1]

The last paragraph is so characteristic of the Roman Catholic, and is common also to the Hindoo. It is the expiatory system—confession and Mass will cover any indulgence in even what they call mortal sin. Newman says in his 'Lectures on Certain Difficulties felt by Anglicans in submitting to the Catholic Church,' No. ix., p. 240:

'The poor Protestant adds sin to sin, and his best aspirations come to nothing; the Catholic wipes off his guilt again and again, and even if his repentance does not endure, and he has not strength to persevere, in a certain sense he is never getting worse, but ever beginning afresh. . . . Let death come suddenly upon him, and let him have the preparation of a poor hour—what is the Protestant to do? He has nothing but sights of this world around him—wife, and children, and friends, and worldly interests; the Catholic has these also, but the Protestant has nought but these. . . . The Catholic has within him almost

[1] Vol. ii., p. 342.

a principle of recovery, certainly an instrument of it. He may have spoken lightly of the Almighty, but he has ever believed in Him; he has sung jocose songs about the Blessed Virgin and Saints, and told good stories about the evil spirit, but in levity, not in contempt; he has been angry with his heavenly patrons when things went ill with him, but with the waywardness of a child who is cross with his parents. . . . He has absented himself from his Easter duties years out of number, but he has never denied he was a Catholic. He has laughed at priests, and formed rash judgments of them, and slandered them to others, but not as doubting the divinity of their functions, and the virtue of their ministrations. He has attended Mass carelessly and heartlessly, but he was ever aware what was before his eyes, under the veil of material symbols, in that august and adorable action. So, when the news comes to him that he is to die, and he cannot get a priest . . . his thoughts at once take shape and order. . . . He addresses himself to his crucifix; he interests the Blessed Virgin in his behalf; he betakes himself to his patron saints; he calls his good angel to his side; he professes his desire of that sacramental absolution which for circumstances he cannot obtain; he exercises himself in acts of faith, hope, charity, contrition, resignation, and other virtues suitable to his extremity. True, he is going to an unseen world; but true also, that unseen world has already been with him here. True, he is going to a foreign, but not to a strange place; judgment and purgatory are familiar ideas to him, more fully realized within him even than death. He has had a much deeper perception of purgatory, though it be a supernatural object, than of death, though a natural one. The enemy rushes on him to overthrow the faith on which he is built; but the whole tenor of his past life, his very jesting and his very oaths, has been overruled, to create in him a habit of faith, girding round and protecting the supernatural principle. And thus even one who has been a bad Catholic may have a hope in his death, to which the most virtuous of Protestants, nay, my dear brethren, the most correct and most thoughtful among yourselves, however able, or learned, or sagacious, if you have not lived by faith, but by private judgment, are necessarily strangers.'

So the most virtuous Protestant is in an infinitely worse state than the Roman Catholic who has 'spoken lightly of the Almighty,' thus contravening the third commandment; who has joked about the Virgin and Saints; who has told good stories about the devil; who has slandered his priests, thus breaking the ninth commandment; and has neglected his Church. The excuse made for these repeated transgressions is that it is all done in 'levity, and not in contempt.'

Will this excuse avail him at the Last Day, when he finds that his knowledge of the unseen world is nothing but the purest ignorance, and that the purgatory of which he had such a 'deep perception' is non-existent?

No wonder Newman's friends thought he was out of his mind, when he could descend to such teaching as this. It was in his case that 'much learning had made him mad.'

In his 'Apologia pro Vitâ suâ' (ed. 1890), p. 168, he says:

'Or it might so happen that my head got simply confused by the very strength of the logic which was administered to me, and thus I gave my sanction to conclusions which really were not mine.'

Surely this must have been the case in this lecture.

Meanwhile, we leave Newman and Manning saying Masses for each other.

CHAPTER XV.

TWO years later, on November 3, 1869, Newman wrote to Manning:

'Thank you for your kind letter. I can only repeat what I said when you last heard from me: I do not know whether I am on my head or my heels when I have active relations with you. In spite of my friendly feelings, this is the judgment of my intellect.'[1]

On this letter Manning comments in an autobiographical note:

'His last was in terms which made a reply hardly fitting on my part. For years we never wrote and never met.'[2]

Manning, however, had written, on the same day (November 3, 1869) on which Newman wrote to him, to the Bishop of Birmingham:

'... My belief is that some persons have come between Dr. Newman and myself. I have borne this

[1] Vol. ii., p. 346. [2] *Ibid.*

so long as it was only a private pain. But it has become a public danger to our peace, and to the fair name of the Catholic religion ; and my purpose is to pursue it, till I find the authors who write anonymously.'[1]

As we have seen, he had not far to go to 'find the authors.' He himself was responsible for the open attacks made on Newman, and for those made anonymously he supplied Talbot with the material.

The following extracts from five letters written by Talbot to Manning show ' development ' :

July 23, 1867.—' You have heard by this time that Dr. Neve has resigned his post of Rector of the English College.'[2]

August 31, 1867.—' I have received no answer to my letter in which I informed your Grace that Dr. Neve had, of his own accord, resigned the Rectorship of the English College.'[3]

September 17, 1867.—' I know no one who sees through character better than the Holy Father himself. He saw through Dr. Neve long before I did, and could not conceive why he had been proposed by the English Bishops.'[4]

September 27, 1867.—' Dr. Neve is awfully sulky, but he really has no hardship to complain of. He has brought it all on himself.'[5]

[1] Vol. ii., p. 344. [2] Vol. ii., p. 368. [3] Vol. ii., p. 369.
[4] Vol. ii., p. 370. [5] Vol. ii., p. 371.

November 13, 1867.—' Dr. Neve is going about Rome grumbling as usual, and attributes motives which do not exist.'[1]

To this last letter Manning replied :

' Never mind the arch-grumbler, but do not send him to h . . v . n.'[2]

What did Manning mean by this last? Was he, like Newman's ' bad Catholic,' making jests of serious things ? or was it that his 'keen insight into the invisible world' led him not to believe in it at all?

' Familiarity breeds contempt ' is truer in this connection than in anything else.

We now take leave of Monsignor Talbot.

As we have already quoted, he ' used to complain that, when no longer needing his help, Archbishop Manning neglected him,'[3] so now we are told ' Monsignor Talbot's reason gave way, and he was removed to an asylum at Passy, near Paris, and died there in 1886. In all Manning's Diaries, Journals, and Reminiscences there is no record or mention of Monsignor Talbot's illness and death. His letters . . . suddenly came to an end in 1868. Henceforth, Monsignor Talbot's name disappears, sinks out of sight as a stone cast into the waters.'[4]

The next great event in Manning's life was the Vatican Council, in which he bore such a promi-

---

[1] Vol. ii., p. 376.
[2] Vol. ii., p. 376.
[3] Vol. ii., p. 696. note.
[4] Vol. ii., p. 485.

nent part, and which he describes in the following terms :

'The public history of the Council I have given in the "True Story." The private history is known to few. Ratisbon, Carcassonne, Malines, Paderborn, and I began meeting in order to watch and counteract the French and the German Bishops who were united in an international committee. We met at my rooms, and Ratisbon's, and Paderborn's rooms, and finally at the Villa Caserta. One day the opposition came and half filled the room ; we had to adjourn. In the end we drew up the *postulatum* asking that the definition should be proposed to the Council. The whole is told in the "True Story." I remember our anxiety while the signatures were coming in, hindered and delayed by intrigue and misrepresentation ; and finally, when the *postulatum* came before the *deputatio de postulatis*. It was a Sunday morning. We met in the Vatican. Out of twenty-five, all but two or three voted to recommend the Holy Father that the Definition should be proposed to the Council. This was the first great step in advance. The International Committee met often, and we met weekly to watch and to counteract. When they went to Pius IX., we went also. It was a running fight. . . . On the secret history of the *deputatio de fide*, see a Latin memorandum by the Bishop of Ratisbon, of which no use must be made while Cardinal Bilio lives, nor, after his death, in any way to dim the great name of one whom I love much.'¹

And further :

'Nothing is too base for the partisan spirit. I understand now the confusion which prevailed, and the misunderstanding that darkened the minds of men in too many a council. The calumnies of yesterday were not one whit worse than those of to-day. Cowardice in weak and well-meaning men is but too common in every age, and so are bribery and corruption, fraud and falsehood.'²

This is an extraordinary account of a meeting of Cardinals and Bishops of the one Catholic Church that has 'Divine life' and 'Divine reality in its acts.' Are these the holy confessors and directors of souls to whom are imputed 'bribery and corruption, fraud and falsehood'?

But in his 'True Story of the Vatican Council,' published in 1877, Manning said :

'No one who has watched with any attention the pontificate of Pius IX. will believe that the definition of the infallibility of the Roman Pontiff was the work of any parties or intrigues' (p. 41).

'Inasmuch as the arguments which were weighing in the minds of Bishops for and against the opportuneness of defining this doctrine were not—as controversialists, politicians, newspapers, and the religious

¹ Vol. ii., p. 453.   ² Vol. ii., p. 453.

adversaries of the Church would have men believe—arbitrary, factious, contentious, intriguing, servile, or unreasoning' (p. 100).

'Not only acts that were never done, words that were never spoken, motives that were never thought of, were imputed to those of the majority whose duty forced them to choose truth before popularity' (p. 140).

'There was no concealment or intrigue on either side; it was needed by neither; it would have been worse than useless if it had been attempted' (p. 158).

'It was a fair trial of reason, argument and legitimate strength' (p. 159).

How are these two accounts to be reconciled?

Do Newman's words in his 'Lectures on Certain Difficulties felt by Anglicans in submitting to the Catholic Church,' xi., p. 286 (ed. 1890) apply here?

'And surely we can fancy without difficulty the circumstances in which a people and their priesthood, who ought to hinder it, may gradually fall into those heavy and sluggish habits of mind, in which faith is but material, and obedience mechanical, and religion has become a superstition instead of a reasonable service; and then it is as certain that they will become schismatics or heretics, should trial come, as that infidel cities, which have no heart for the truth, when it is for the first time preached to them, will remain in their infidelity. It is much to be feared, from what travellers tell us of the Greek priesthood and their flocks, that both in Russia and in Greece proper they are very much in this state—what may be called the proper disposition towards heresy and schism. I mean that they rely on things more than on persons, and go through a round of duties, in one and the same way, because they are used to them, not as having any intelligent faith in a Divine oracle which has ordered them; and that in consequence they would start in irritation, as they have started, from such indication of that oracle's existence as is necessarily implied in a new definition of faith.'

He seems exactly to have fitted the case, only, instead of priests and people, it should be Cardinals and Bishops.

'The misunderstanding that darkened the minds of men in too many a council.' For 'men' read 'Bishops.' Does Manning mean by this to throw over the decrees of any of the Councils? Had he the Council of Trent in his mind? Did he remember its composition?

We shall understand the tenderness towards Cardinal Bilio when we come to record the doings of the Conclave after the death of Pius IX. What would Manning's perverts have thought of this description of the acts and motives of the highest Council of the Church? Would not Newman have withdrawn his lectures to Anglicans, had he seen this?

The Vatican Council decreed the dogma of Papal Infallibility on July 18, 1870; but the interest excited by such an event was to a great extent neutralized by the declaration of war by France against Prussia on the following day. And now, with this account by one who was there, and who took a prominent part in the Council, we should think Roman Catholics would willingly wash their hands of the whole matter. At any rate, Nemesis was swift, as in September of that same year (1870) the temporal power of the Pope ceased for ever.

We next have to chronicle some of the compliments that passed between the higher officials of the One, True, Indivisible, Catholic Church. 'Manning was described by them (the Cardinals) as "Il diplomatico," Clifford as "Il avvocato," and Vaughan as "Il diavolo." It was retorted on them that talking with Cardinals in Rome was like talking to owls at noonday.'[1]

Newman told us, 'When I became a Catholic nothing struck me more at once than the English outspoken manner of the priests.'[2]

But even he could not have expected it would go as far as this. Of course, he was trying to excuse them from the charges he himself had made against them in the *British Critic*, 1840. And to quote the same author again:

[1] Vol. ii., p. 508.
[2] 'Apologia pro Vitâ suâ,' ed. 1890, p. 271.

' Her [the Church's] best fruit is necessarily secret. She fights with the heart of man; her perpetual conflict is against the pride, the impurity, the covetousness, the envy, the animosity, which never gets so far as to come to light, which she succeeds in strangling in its birth.'[1] But in this case the fruit is not secret. It has come to light, and 'pride, covetousness, envy, and animosity' are manifested by 'calumny, bribery, corruption, fraud, and falsehood.' If such be the shepherds, in what condition are the sheep? Again: 'The Church aims at realities, the world at decencies; she dispenses with a complete work, so she can but make a thorough one.'[2] In this case the work had neither been complete nor thorough. Even the decency of the world was dispensed with.

Manning was made a Cardinal on March 15, 1875, and in the following year, on the death of Cardinal Antonelli, the Papal Secretary of State, proceeded to Rome, and Mr. Purcell tells us:

'Of all the Pope's advisers, no one was more urgent than Cardinal Manning in insisting upon the absolute necessity—in the interests of the Church, for the sake of the Temporal Power, for the safeguarding of the liberty and spiritual rights of the Papacy—of finding a great ecclesiastical statesman as successor to Cardinal

---

[1] 'Lectures on Certain Difficulties felt by Anglicans in submitting to the Catholic Church,' ix., p. 219.
[2] *Ibid.*, viii., p. 208.

Antonelli. Carried away by his zeal, and relying on the latitude, in offering advice, allowed him by Pius IX., Cardinal Manning criticized very freely the qualifications of the few available candidates for the office of Secretary of State. He even hinted at the stagnation in the Sacred College; its want of a common understanding, of prevision, of resourcefulness. Finally, at the conclusion of his interview with Pope Pius IX., Cardinal Manning, in sorrow of heart, lamented that, at a moment when a great ecclesiastical statesman was most needed, the Holy See was most wanting in its councillors and men of action. Soon after this interview, Cardinal Manning complained to an intimate friend that " Pope Pius IX. was growing old and garrulous, and not to be trusted with a secret." What was the secret which the Pope betrayed? Did Pope Pius IX., yielding to his love of a practical joke, introduce Cardinal Manning to a rival and astounded Cardinal as " Antonelli il secondo "? It was not till the succeeding year that Cardinal Nina—the astounded Cardinal—was appointed Secretary of State.'[1]

Manning now felt the loss of his quasi-friend. 'Whispers' were no longer forthcoming on his behalf. Manning was still true to his principles; he did not 'ask for' anything; he did not 'canvass,' but he blackened the character of all possible rivals. Perhaps the Pope, who, as Talbot told Manning in Dr. Neve's

[1] Vol. ii., p. 573.

case in 1867, 'saw through characters quicker than anybody else,' had at last discovered the true character of Manning's methods and ambitions.

In his letter to a penitent on June 1, 1865, Manning had described the Holy Father as 'the most supernatural person I have ever seen.' How had he fallen from this high estate to be 'growing old and garrulous, and not to be trusted with a secret'? Manning in the same letter had said : 'If anything has consoled me it is the feeling that, if the Vicar of our Lord trusts me, our Lord does not distrust me.' Of course the converse would be equally true. 'If the Vicar of our Lord distrusts me, our Lord distrusts me.' But, no. Manning goes away to Genoa, and there writes his 'impressions' on December 8, 1876 :

'. . . (5) Still more of the Sacred College. At least seven or eight of the men I remember in full vigour are partially or wholly useless. They still nominally hold their office.

'. . . (8) I seemed to see stagnation. Six years have passed over the Holy See since 1870, and its organization has been dying out year after year.

'(9) I seemed also to see that there is no common counsel, no common understanding, no preparation, no provision, no readiness for alternatives.

'(10) I find some looking for miracles, (2) some for inaction, (3) some for action. Therefore there is no unity of mind.'[1]

This is a somewhat trenchant criticism of the Sacred College, and it would be profanation on our part to improve upon it. Manning evidently did not believe in miracles. He had been too long behind the scenes not to know how they were effected. He believed in 'action' first; and then when that action has taken effect, he could ascribe the results of it to supernatural means. The greatest miracle that could have happened, in Manning's view, would have been that he should have been appointed Secretary of State. Had he been so appointed, no doubt we should have had to record letters of the same tenor as those sent to penitents and others on his appointment to the archbishopric of Westminster. Manning had not the 'simple faith' of Newman, or he would hardly have passed reflections on the members of the Sacred College for sitting and waiting for miracles.

Newman says:

'It is plain that there is nothing extravagant in the report of her [St. Walburga] relics having a supernatural virtue; and for this reason, because there are such instances in Scripture, and Scripture cannot be extravagant. For instance, a man was restored to life by touching the relics of the Prophet Elisha.

[1] Vol. ii., p. 575.

Again in the case of an inanimate substance which had touched a living saint. "And God wrought *special miracles;* by the hands of Paul; so that *from his body* were brought unto the sick *handkerchiefs or aprons*, and the diseases departed from them."[1]

We must illustrate this by a further quotation from the same author:

'Nothing is more to be expected in large populations of Christians, if left to themselves, than a material instead of a formal faith. By a material faith, I mean that sort of habitual belief, which persons possess in consequence of having heard things said in this or that way from their childhood, being thoroughly familiar with them, and never having had difficulty suggested to them from without or within. Such is the sort of belief which many Protestants have in the Bible; which they accept without a doubt, till objections occur to them. Such as this becomes the faith of nations in time, where a clergy is negligent; it becomes simply material and hereditary, the truth being received, but not on the authority of God. That is, their faith is but material, not formal, and really has neither the character nor the reward of that grace-implanted, grace-sustained principle, which believes, not merely because it was taught so in the nursery, but because God has spoken, not because there is no temptation to doubt, but

[1] 'Apologia pro Vitâ suâ,' ed. 1890, p. 300.

because there is a duty to believe' ('Lectures on Certain Difficulties felt by Anglicans in submitting to the Catholic Church,' xi., p. 284).

These two extracts explain a great deal that would perhaps be otherwise incomprehensible in the character of Roman Catholics. They have 'heard from their childhood' and are 'thoroughly familiar' with the legends of the saints; they are acquainted with the special days set apart in honour of those saints; they are carefully taught the benefit of pilgrimages to the shrines of those saints, and the miracles to be effected there; they are forbidden to read books which may cast doubts on the reality of the saint or the miracles; they are strictly taught that it is a duty to believe. And all this because the clergy are *not* negligent. The 'poor Protestant' (or the Anglican divines, to whom these lectures were delivered) is told that he has not formal faith if he cannot believe in these miracles. There is nothing extravagant about them, as miracles of the same description are recorded in Scripture. There was nothing extravagant in the Pope assuming the name of the 'Lord God' in his celebrated *coup d'état*. There was nothing extravagant in Manning assuming the character of St. Paul when he stood by the side of Mr. Gladstone at the last service at which he took part in the English Church. It is only the 'keen insight into the invisible world' which the Roman Catholics possess. The Spiritualists, too, claim this, and have performed their miracles, but they have unfortunately been found out. It is this material faith, and the objective worship consequent thereon, that caused Talbot to describe Rome as the 'source and centre of ambition and intrigue'; that caused Manning to write such a description of the Vatican Council; that caused Manning to write to Talbot not to 'send the arch-grumbler [Dr. Neve] to h .. v . n'; and that has been the cause of all the bloody wars and massacres that Rome is responsible for.

Pius IX. died in 1878, and Manning, describing the Conclave that took place after the Pope's death, says in an autobiographical note:

'Bilio said that he considered it necessary in the present conflict of the Church that the next Pope should be a foreigner, and then suggested myself.'[1]

We thus have the explanation of the special tenderness that is to be shown to Cardinal Bilio, or his memory, when the full description of the inner working of the Vatican Council comes to be written.

In another autobiographical note, 'in repudiation of most offensive statements in Bishop Wilberforce's Diary, imputing to Manning abject servility in lying prostrate "at the Pope's feet, and refusing to rise," and adulation by flattering the vanity of Pope Pius IX. in regard to Papal Infallibility,

[1] Vol. ii., p. 550.

Cardinal Manning wrote: "I speak the truth in Christ and lie not, my conscience also bearing witness in the Holy Ghost, that neither in Pius IX. nor in me were such thoughts and motions as poor Samuel Wilberforce had the heart to conceive."[1]

Was this note dictated by St. Alphonsus' principles? Is there any 'ambiguity' here?

Peter denied his Lord, and on the third occasion began to curse and to swear.

Manning had many enemies both at Rome and in England, and no doubt 'poor Samuel Wilberforce' had full authority for what he had stated in his Diary.

Mr. Purcell tells us:

'During the Pontiff's lifetime, at the opening of the Church of St. Dominic at Newcastle, Cardinal Manning, in his enthusiasm, professed his belief "that when the history of the Pontificate of Pius IX. shall be written, it will be found to have been one of the most resplendent, majestic, and powerful—one that has reached over the whole extent of the Church with greater power than that of any other Pope in the whole succession." Had he been alive at the time, Bishop Wilberforce might, perhaps, with some reason, have objected to a eulogy so premature and unlimited.'[2]

---

[1] Vol. ii., p. 551.   [2] Vol. ii., p. 553.

CHAPTER XVI.

WE now have to complete the story of Manning's relations to Newman.

'In the summer of 1878, not six months after Leo XIII.'s accession, Newman's friends were taking active steps to bring his unrivalled services to religion and the Catholic Church in England under the special attention of the new Pope.'[1]

Newman had now been for thirty-three years a member of the Church of Rome, and the only promotion he had received during that long period had been to the priorship of the Oratory of Birmingham. The movement was initiated by the Roman Catholic laity, and the Duke of Norfolk and Lord Ripon on their behalf had an interview with Cardinal Manning.

'On hearing the proposal, Cardinal Manning bent his head, and remained silent for some moments. Recovering his self-possession, he rose to the occasion. With great alacrity he offered to embody in a letter of

[1] Vol. ii., p. 554.

his own to Cardinal Nina the substance of the statements drawn up or indicated by the Duke of Norfolk and Lord Ripon, together with the various reasons which they had brought forward in support of their petition.'[1]

Manning again rose to the occasion.

'Early in December [1878], Cardinal Howard, to whom Cardinal Manning had entrusted his letter containing the reasons which induced English laymen to hope that Father Newman would be made a Cardinal, not having arrived in Rome, the Duke of Norfolk sought a private audience with Pope Leo XIII. In a letter dated "Ambassador d'Angleterre, Paris, December 12, 1878," the Duke of Norfolk urged Cardinal Manning, as his first letter was now out of date, owing to Cardinal Howard's delay on his journey, to write again to Rome, and to reiterate what he had said before. After giving an account of his private audience with Leo XIII., the Duke of Norfolk added that the Pope seemed to think the request to make Father Newman a Cardinal, coming from laymen, a high-reaching one, but seemed willing to consider it. The Duke of Norfolk added that the Pope asked particularly what Cardinal Manning thought of the matter. The Duke of Norfolk's statements, giving an account of the strange way in which Newman had been so long neglected and mistrusted,

[1] Vol. ii., p. 555.

made a strong impression on Pope Leo XIII. The presentation at last of Cardinal Manning's letter by Cardinal Howard served to confirm the favourable impression, and to supply what may have been wanting in regularity in the Duke of Norfolk's request. At the end of January a letter was written by Cardinal Nina to Cardinal Manning to the effect that Pope Leo XIII. had "intimated his desire to raise Dr. Newman to the rank of Cardinal."[1]

On February 5, 1879, Newman wrote to Manning:

'Thank you for sending me your rough copy. I could not be so ungracious, whether to the Holy Father, or to the friends at home who have interested themselves in this matter, as to decline what was so kindly proposed, provided that it did not involve unfaithfulness to St. Philip.'[2]

'On Saturday, February 15, 1879, Cardinal Manning, bearing Newman's answer to Cardinal Nina, started for Rome. He passed through Paris, where he remained a day or two. From the following correspondence it appears that Cardinal Manning, from the perusal of the letters to Cardinal Nina, to himself, and to the Bishop of Birmingham, had fully persuaded himself that Newman had declined to accept the dignity of Cardinal. Such a belief was by no means shared by the Bishop of Birmingham or the Duke of Norfolk. By a strange error of judgment, almost un-

[1] Vol. ii., p. 557.   [2] Vol. ii., p. 560.

accountable in one so distinguished for his prudence and sense of propriety, Cardinal Manning, as appears from Newman's letter to the Duke of Norfolk, not only divulged the fact that the dignity of Cardinal had been offered, but, putting his own interpretation on the letter to Cardinal Nina, unfortunately before even the letter had reached its destination in Rome, allowed the statement to be made public that Newman had refused the Pope's offer. Unquestionably Cardinal Manning had deceived himself as to the true meaning of Newman's letter to Cardinal Nina, but did his best on reaching Rome to repair his error. In the meantime, the following statement appeared in the *Times* of Tuesday, February 18, 1879 :

'" Pope Leo XIII. has intimated his desire to raise Dr. Newman to the rank of Cardinal; but, with expressions of deep respect for the Holy See, Dr. Newman has excused himself from accepting the purple."

'On reading this Father Newman wrote to the Duke of Norfolk :

'" I have heard from various quarters of the affectionate interest you have taken in the application to Rome about me, and I write to thank you, and to express my great pleasure at it. As to the statement of my refusing a Cardinal's hat, which is in the papers, you must not believe it—for this reason : of course it implies that an offer has been made me, and I have sent an answer to it. Now, I have ever understood that it is a point of propriety and honour to consider such communications *sacred*. The statement, therefore, cannot come from me. Nor could it come from Rome, for it was made public before my answer got to Rome. It could only come, then, from someone who not only read my letter, but, instead of leaving to the Pope to interpret it, took upon himself to put an interpretation upon it, and published that interpretation to the world. A private letter, addressed to the Roman authorities, is interpreted on its way, and published in the English papers. How is it possible that anyone can have done this? And besides, I am quite sure that, if so high an honour was offered me, I should not answer it by a blunt refusal."[1]

'As soon as Newman's letter to the Duke of Norfolk reached Cardinal Manning in Rome, he hastened to explain how his interpretation of Newman's letter to Cardinal Nina differed from Newman's own interpretation. Cardinal Nina, after listening to Cardinal Manning's explanation, dryly remarked that the author was usually a better interpreter than another of his own words. With Pope Leo XIII. there was no difficulty. With sympathetic insight he fully entered into Newman's feelings, and highly appreciated the delicacy he had shown in his letter to Cardinal Nina. Without hesitation or delay Pope Leo conferred on Father Newman the dignity of

[1] Vol. ii., p. 560.

Cardinal, and gladly gave him the privilege he desired of remaining in England with his brethren at the Oratory.'[1]

Cardinal Manning gives his explanation to Newman in a letter written from Rome on March 8, 1879:

'Your second letter has just reached me. Mine will have been received before this, and you will know that I have not a second time failed to understand your intention. The letter written by you to the Bishop of Birmingham, in answer to Cardinal Nina's letter, was sent by the Bishop to me with a letter of his own. I fully believed that, for the reasons given in your letter, you declined what might be offered. But the Bishop expressed his hope that you might, under a change of conditions, accept it. This confirmed my belief that, as it stood, you declined it. And your letter to me of a day or two later still further confirmed my belief. I started for Rome taking with me the Bishop's letter, not knowing what might be done here. In passing through Paris I wrote to the Duke of Norfolk in the sense I have written above. I never doubted this impression, received from your letters and the Bishop's, till I received from the Duke a copy of a letter of yours to him, in which you said you had not intended to refuse what had been proposed. The moment I read this I went to the Vatican,

[1] Vol. ii., p. 566.

and told the Holy Father, and asked his permission to write to the Duke and to the Bishop of Birmingham. And to shorten still further the suspense, I telegraphed to both. I write this because, if I misunderstood your intention, it was by an error which I repaired the instant I knew it.'[1]

A very insufficient and 'ambiguous' explanatory statement. Manning's 'aims and methods' can be distinctly traced all through this piece of intrigue. Disliking the proposal when he first hears of it, Manning, with his 'forecasting temperament,' planned his line of action, and 'with great alacrity' offered to send a letter to Rome. There is no doubt that Cardinal Howard, to whom the letter was intrusted, had full instructions to delay on his journey as much as possible; but Manning had misconceived the persistency of Newman's partisans. The Duke of Norfolk not only pleads Newman's cause in an audience with the Pope, but actually writes to Manning, asking him to write a second letter to Rome, '*as his first letter was now out of date.*' The offer of a Cardinal's hat is then made to Newman.

But Manning's resources are not yet exhausted. He receives Newman's answer, and starts with it for Rome, but stops in Paris on the way, and the third day after he has left England the statement of Newman's refusal appears in the *Times*. The premature

[1] Vol. ii., p. 568.

publication of this statement, before Newman's answer had been received in Rome, was calculated not only to seriously offend the Pope, but to put a stop to any further action on the part of Newman's friends. There is no question of an 'error of judgment,' or of Manning's having 'deceived himself.' Had the Pope been Pius IX., and had the 'whisperer' been at hand, Manning might have been successful; but he now realized the truth of Newman's words, 'Craft and cruelty, and whatever is base and wicked, have a sure Nemesis, and eventually strike the heads of those who are guilty of them' (letter to the *Times*, September, 1872). Cardinal Newman died in 1890, and at the solemn requiem held at the Oratory, South Kensington, on August 20, Cardinal Manning gave the address:

'When these tidings came to me, my first thought was this: In what way can I, once more, show my love and veneration for my brother and friend of more than sixty years? . . . Someone has said, "Whether Rome canonizes him or not, he will be canonized in the thoughts of pious people of many creeds in England." . . . A noble and beautiful life is the most convincing of all preaching, and we have all felt its power.'[1]

Mr. Purcell's comments on this address are very much to the point:

[1] Vol. ii., p. 749.

'In the opening passage of his address, Cardinal Manning drew a most touching and pathetic picture of his relations with John Henry Newman, which he described as "a friendship of sixty years and more." In the emotion of the moment, under the stress of conflicting memories, in the agitation which he could not but feel, and which he showed at making history, as it were, in the face of the world, Cardinal Manning, perhaps not unnaturally, forgot his prolonged opposition to Newman in Rome and in England; forgot his avowed hostility and mistrust; forgot that for half a century—from 1840 to 1890—he had not met or spoken to Newman more than half a dozen times. At Littlemore they met but once, and once at the Oratory in Birmingham. As Cardinals, they met but twice—for the first time in June, 1883, at Archbishop's House at Westminster, and their second and last meeting was in 1884, at Birmingham. Manning and Newman were never intimate, either early or late in life — not at Oriel or at Littlemore, nor at the Oratory in Birmingham. Apart from a few letters of congratulation, or courtesy, or explanatory notes, all correspondence or communication between Newman and Manning ceased in 1866. . . . At that supreme moment, the not unnatural desire of Manning's heart was that his name should go forth before the world, linked with that of Newman as a lifelong friend and fellow-worker — that he might, in a sense, be a co-partner in Newman's glory.'[1]

Newman, in his 'Lectures on Certain Difficulties felt by Anglicans in submitting to the Catholic Church,' Lecture x., on ' Differences among Catholics no Prejudice to the Unity of the Catholic Church,' p. 251, says :

' When Catholics in any country are poor or few, each religious body, each college, each priest, is tempted to do his utmost for himself at the expense of everyone else. I do not mean for his temporal interests, for he has not the temptation, but for the interests of his own mission, and place, and of his own people. . . . All parties then are naturally led to look out for themselves in the first instance, and this state of mind may easily degenerate into a jealousy of the good fortune or prosperity of others. And then again, some men, or races of men, are more sudden in their tempers than others, or individuals may be deficient in moral training or refinement, and strangers may mistake for a real dissension what is nothing more than momentary and transitory collision.'

Newman could not have written this at the close of his career in the Church of Rome. Manning's animosity never ceased from the day that he became a Roman Catholic. Newman was a possible 'stumbling-block in his path,' and had to be 'cautiously and

[1] Vol. ii., p. 752.

gradually removed.' As Talbot wrote, 'His spirit must be crushed.' But to finish with this eulogium, false on his part at least, showed a depth of hypocrisy that can scarcely be credited.

We have a few more details of Cardinal Manning's life. In 'Reflections,' written at Florence, December 4, 1883, Manning says:

'In talking about Ireland in my first audience [with Leo XIII., in 1883], I said that the preservation of the Imperial Unity is vital to the three kingdoms, and to Ireland above all. The Holy Father seemed to be relieved, as if he expected Home Rule from me.'[1]

But, 'On the introduction of Gladstone's Home Rule Bill in 1886, Cardinal Manning expressed his cordial concurrence with the provisions it made for granting to the Irish people the fullest right to manage their own local or domestic concerns, but he regarded as a fatal objection to the Bill the transference of the Irish members from Westminster to a Parliament in Dublin. In his pleasant and friendly way he told the Irish Catholic members that he could not spare one of them from the Parliament of the United Kingdom; naturally he did not tell them, as he had told the Pope, that a Parliament at Dublin meant separation from England. . . . It must be remembered in this connection that Cardinal Manning was in the habit of drawing a distinction between views and principles

[1] Vol. ii., p. 579.

which he had avowed in public, and views or sympathies which he entertained in private. Littera scripta manet. But unavowed views might, owing to the course of events, undergo modification or change, or be altogether dropped. . . . It was only in 1887 that Cardinal Manning avowed himself a Home Ruler.'[1]

Double-facedness had been of inestimable benefit to Manning during the whole course of his life. He had always run with the hare and hunted with the hounds ; he had watched how 'the land lay,' and then chosen his course accordingly.

The Pope evidently, like Newman, did not 'know whether he was on his head or his heels' when talking to Manning.

Newman, in his 'Apologia pro Vitâ suâ,' ed. 1890, p. 270, had quoted three 'Rules of Economy,' which Manning had not only taken to heart, but had even improved upon :

'1. Concealing the truth when we could do so without deceit.
'2. Stating it only partially.
'3. Representing it under the nearest form possible to a learner or inquirer, when he could not possibly understand it exactly.'

Had Newman forgotten that 'falsehood generally rests on a partial or perverted truth'?

[1] Vol. ii., p. 617.

Perhaps the Irish Catholic Members were 'learners' or 'inquirers,' and came under Rule 3.

We next have Manning's change of views on the Temporal Power of the Pope.

'The loss of faith, the loss of religion among the rising generation of the people of Italy, he accounted as a greater evil than the loss of the Temporal Power of the Pope.'[1]

'After this change of front in regard to the Temporal Power, strained relations took the place of former friendly feelings between the ruling Cardinals and Cardinal Manning. The Jesuits in Rome regarded the former champion of the Temporal Power of the Pope as a renegade to his principles.'[2]

'On being reminded that he was turning his back on the principles which for the last twenty years he had held in defence of the Temporal Power of the Pope, his enigmatical reply was, "I am beginning to feel my feet in the Italian question."'[3]

What are we now to think of Newman's eulogy of the 'Catholic population of Italy'?

They had weighed the 'Catholic Church' in the balance, and found it wanting.

Manning, too, was coming out in his true colours. He had been a supporter of that Church for nearly forty years, and yet he is only 'beginning to feel his feet in the Italian question.'

[1] Vol. ii., p. 611. [2] Vol. ii., p. 614. [3] Vol. ii., p. 615.

CHAPTER XVII.

THERE is a mysterious autobiographical note on April 19, 1889:

'And so I fear it will be in Italy. The abdication of natural duty called abstention, is not the mind of the Holy See, but of him that letteth, and will let until he be broken out of the way. Quousque Domine?'[1]

Was it the Pope who was described as 'him that letteth'? Or was it Cardinal Nina? The 'mind of the Holy See' does not mean the mind of the Pope, but what the individual Roman Catholic — in this case Manning—thinks ought to be the 'mind of the Holy See.'

Here the Pope is forbidding the Roman Catholics to record their votes in any elections in Italy. And when the Pope issued a decree condemning the 'Plan of Campaign,' Manning, after acknowledging that the Infallible Magisterium Romani Pontificis extends over politics, writes in his Journal, 1890:

[1] Vol. ii., p. 617.

'But is there in this no limit? Now, as there is no action which is not either good or bad in the agent, so there is nothing indifferent in the action of the Commonwealth. It is therefore undeniable that the Pontiffs were morally within their right in the Crusades, the Armada, and in the condemnation of boycotting and the Plan of Campaign, let alone the Parnell Testimonial. But it is one thing to be morally right or not morally wrong, and another altogether to be within natural and supernatural prudence. I have been always unable to think certain of these acts to be prudent. It is easy to be wise after the event. But the event seems to have pronounced against them. . . . Pontiffs have no infallibility of the world of facts, except only dogmatic. And prudence is the first of the cardinal virtues.'[1]

Is it 'undeniable that the Pontiffs were morally within their right in the Crusades and the Armada'? It is a curious commentary on the protestations made by the Roman Catholics before the passing of the 'Catholic Emancipation' Bill, to find a Cardinal of the Roman Catholic Church, and an Englishman to boot, stating as an undeniable fact that the Pope was morally within his right in stirring up the King of Spain to launch the Armada against this country. Where was that Pope's Christianity? Where was Manning's Christianity? He not only condones the

[1] Vol. ii., p. 625.

act, but approves the principle, and only considers it was not 'altogether within natural and supernatural prudence,' as shown by the event. How little Newman knew of the real Church of Rome, when he ventured to address the Anglican divines on their difficulties in submitting to the 'Catholic Church'!

'What a vast assemblage of private feeling, judgment, taste, and tradition goes to make up the idea of nationality! Yet there it exists in the Church, because the Church has not been divinely instructed to forbid it, and it fights against the Church, and the Church's objects, except where the Church authoritatively repels it. The Church is a preacher of peace, and nationality is the fruitful cause of quarrels far more sinful and destructive than the paper wars and rivalry of customs or precedents, which alone can possibly exist between religious bodies. The Church grants to the magistrate the power of the sword, and the right of making war in a lawful quarrel, and nations abuse this prerogative to break up that unity of love which ought to exist in the baptized servants of a common Master, and to put to death by wholesale those whom they expect to live with for ever in heaven. . . . Look through her [the Church's] history, and you cannot deny that she is the one great principle of unity and concord which the world has seen. . . .' Such, too, was her continual arbitration between the fierce feudal monarchs of the Middle Ages; which, though not always successful to the extent of her desires, exhibits her most signally in that her great and heavenly character of peacemaker, and vindicates for her the attribute, given her in the Creed, and envied her by her enemies, of being one' (Lectures on Certain Difficulties,' etc., x., p. 249).

'The Church is a preacher of peace.' It does not practise as it preaches, as we have seen. Was it a 'preacher of peace' in the case of the Armada? But perhaps Newman only meant that 'the Church' was a preacher of peace among those that belonged to its own sect. Of course no mercy is to be shown to heretics. They are to be exterminated, if possible, as we have shown in our extract from the *Analecta Ecclesiastica* for April, 1895. The Roman Catholic Church is responsible for more bloodshed and misery in the world than any mere question of nationality. Instead of being the peacemaker, she has been the inciter to wars and rebellions, whenever it suited her purpose; she has inaugurated massacres and assassinations, and she instituted that most fiendish device of the devil, the Inquisition.

As to her 'continual arbitration between the fierce feudal monarchs of the middle ages,' we will quote Newman against himself. In Lecture VI., p. 150, he says:

'The remarks I have been making are well illustrated by the history of our own great St. Thomas in his contest with King Henry II. Deserted by his suffragans, and threatened with assassination, he is forced to escape, as he can, to the Continent. He puts his cause before the Pope, but with no immediate result, for the Pope is in contest with the Emperor, who has taken part with a pretender to the Apostolic See. For two years nothing is done; then the Pope begins to move, but mediates between the Archbishop and the King, instead of taking the part of the former. The King of France comes forward on the Saint's side, and his friends attempt to gain the Empress Matilda also. Strengthened by these demonstrations, St. Thomas excommunicates some of the King's party, and threatens the King himself, not to say his realm, with an interdict. Then there are appeals to Rome on the part of the King's Bishops, alarmed at the prospect of such extremities, while the Pope gives a more distinct countenance to the Saint's cause. Suddenly the face of things is overcast, the Pope has anathematized the Emperor, and has his hands full of his own matters; Henry's agents at Rome obtain a Legatine Commission under the presidency of a Cardinal favourable to his cause. The quarrel lingers on; two years more have passed, and then the Commission fails. Then St. Thomas rouses himself again, and is proceeding with the interdict, when news comes that the King has overreached the Pope, and the Archbishop's powers are altogether suspended for a set time. The artifice is detected by the good offices of the French Bishops, the Pope sends comminatory letters to the King, but then again does not carry them out. There is a reconciliation between the Kings of England and France at the expense of St. Thomas; but by this time the suspension is over, and the Saint excommunicates the Bishop of London. In consequence he receives a rebuke from the Pope, who, after absolving the Bishop, takes the matter into his own hands, himself excommunicates the Bishop, and himself threatens the kingdom with an interdict. Then St. Thomas returns and is martyred, winning the day by suffering, not by striking.'

Where is the 'heavenly peacemaker' in this piece of Roman Catholic history as narrated by a Roman Catholic?

The 'interdict' meant that all religious services of every description ceased in the country, and that all subjects were absolved from their allegiance in the country affected by it. And yet Newman could tell these Anglican divines in the same lecture (p. 146):

'I repeat the great principles of the State are those of the Church, and if the State would but keep within its own province, it would find the Church its truest ally and best benefactor. She upholds obedience to the magistrate; she recognises his office as from God; she is the preacher of peace, the sanction of law, the first element of order, and the safeguard of morality, and that without possible vacillation or failure; she may be fully trusted ; she is a sure friend ; for she is indefectible and undying.'

And, again, in Lecture VII. (p. 166) he puts it in still stronger terms :

'The Civil Power is a Divine ordinance ; no one doubts it. It is prior to ecclesiastical power. The Jewish lawgivers, judges, prophets, kings had some sort of jurisdiction over the priesthood, though the priesthood had its distinct powers and duties. The Jewish Church was no body distinct from the State. In a certain sense the civil magistrate is what divines call in possession ; the *onus probandi* lies with those who would encroach upon his power. He was in possession in the age when Christ came, he is in possession now in the minds of men, and in the *primâ facie* view of human society. He is in possession, because the benefits he confers on mankind are tangible and obvious to the world at large. And he is recognised and sanctioned in Scripture in the most solemn way ; nay, the very instrument of his power, by which he is strong, is formally committed to him. "Let every soul," says St. Paul, "be subject to higher powers ; for there is no power but from God ; and those that are," the powers that be, "are ordained of God. Therefore he that resisteth the power, resisteth the ordinance of God, and they that resist, purchase to themselves damnation. For princes are not a terror to the good work, but to the evil. Wilt thou, then, not be afraid of the power? Do that which is good, and thou shalt have praise from the same. For he is God's minister to thee for good. But if thou do that which is evil, fear; for he beareth not the sword in vain. For he is God's minister, an avenger to execute wrath upon him that doth evil." It is difficult to find a passage in Scripture more solemn and distinct than this—distinct in the duty laid down, and the sin of transgressing it, and solemn in the reasons on which the duty is enforced. . . . Such is the civil power, the representative, and oracle, and instrument of the eternal law of God, with the power of life and death, the awful power of continuing or cutting short the probation of beings destined to live eternally. To it are committed all things under heaven; it is the sovereign lord of the wide earth, and its various fruits, and of men who till it or traverse it; and it allots and distributes and maintains the one for the benefit of the other. And as it is sacred in its origin, so it may be considered irresponsible in its acts; and treason against it is, as a general rule, rebellion against the Most High.'

How many indictments against the whole Papal system are drawn up in this extract?

If the 'Civil Power is a Divine ordinance,' and 'prior to ecclesiastical power,' how is it that the 'Church grants to the magistrate the power of the sword'? What has the true Church to do with the sword? What did our Lord say on the subject? If the Church grants the power of the sword, she is using the sword, and is responsible.

How came the Pope by his Temporal Power? 'The *onus probandi* lies with those who encroach on the power of the civil magistrate.' And how do they prove it? By a Roman Catholic tradition that sovereign authority over Rome, Italy, and many other provinces of the Western Empire, had been bestowed on Pope Sylvester I. by Constantine the Great, out of gratitude for the baptism which he had received at the hands of that Pope.

Laurentius Valla, a citizen of Rome, in 1441 proved in 'Contra effictam et ementitam Constantini donationem' that for centuries after Constantine's time there was no trace of this tradition, but that it was simply a bold imposture. The Emperor had no power to make such a gift, and the Pope, as the successor of Peter and Vicar of Christ, whose kingdom is not of this world, could not accept such a gift. However, the fact of the gift was pleaded by Adrian I. in a letter to Charlemagne, with the result that he was put in possession of his 'States.' That the 'Church is the safeguard of morality, and that without possible vacillation or failure,' is curious reading after what we have heard of the clergy, seculars and regulars, in Italy.

CHAPTER XVIII.

IN an autobiographical note in 1890 Cardinal Manning writes on the 'hindrances to the spread of Catholicism':

'The confraternities of the Sacred Heart, and the Most Precious Blood, the devotion of the five sacred wounds, the mystery of the Rosary and Crucifix, all are the Gospel in its fulness.'[1]

Newman told us in his 'Apologia pro Vitâ suâ,' p. 196:

'The idea of the Blessed Virgin was, as it were, *magnified* in the Church of Rome, as time went on; but so were all the Christian ideas, as that of the Blessed Eucharist.'

We give some extracts to show the extent of this 'development':

First from '" The Glories of Mary, by St. Alphonso de Liguori, translated from the Italian and carefully revised by a Catholic priest' (Dublin, 1841).

[1] Vol. ii., p. 776.

'The salvation of all depends on preaching devotion to Mary, and confidence in her intercession' (Introd., p. xvii).

'"Yes," says St. Bonaventure, "Mary has so loved us, that she has given us her only Son"' (p. 46).

'The King of Heaven has given us His mother for our Mother, and in her hands resigned (if we might say so) His omnipotence in the sphere of grace; that we might place in her the hope of our salvation, and all the help necessary to attain it' (p. 87).

'"Yes," says Richard of St. Laurence, "Mary is omnipotent; for according to all laws, the Queen enjoys the same privileges as the King; and that power may be equal between the Son and Mother"' (p. 138).

'If the Judge wishes to condemn me, the sentence must pass through this clement Queen, and she well knows how to prevent its execution' (p. 168).

This book, it must be remembered, is one of the works which, according to the Pope and his Council, contained 'nothing worthy of censure.'

Next from Kenrick's 'New Month of Mary' (Dublin, 1841):

'On the assent of the Virgin to the proposition made her hung the destinies of the human race. What would have been our condition if Mary had not yielded this ready compliance with God's will?

We have every reason to conclude that man would not have been redeemed' (p. 62).

'Yes, Holy Mother, if we owe all to Jesus Christ, who has redeemed us, to thee we owe Jesus Himself' (p. 66).

The 'New Month of Mary' is the month of May, as we find from the following:

'The Crown of Jesus: a Complete Catholic Manual of Devotion, Doctrine, and Instruction,' under the sanction of the Cardinal Archbishop of Westminster. 'The devotion of the faithful towards the Mother of God has inspired them to consecrate the month of May in a special manner to her honour. . . . Those who sanctify the month of May by performing every day, either in public or private, some particular devotion in honour of the Blessed Virgin Mary, and by endeavouring to practise some of the virtues of which she has been the model, may gain, each day, Three Hundred Days' Indulgence, and a Plenary Indulgence, on one day at option.'

But the month of May is the month sacred to the pagan goddess of Nature, who was named 'Mylitta' by the Babylonians, 'Isis' by the Egyptians, 'Ishtar' by the Assyrians, 'Astarte' by the Phœnicians, 'Aphrodite' by the Greeks, 'Artemis' and 'Diana' by the Ephesians, 'Venus' by the Romans, 'Holy Mother' by the Chinese, and the 'Queen of Heaven' by Jeremiah. 'Madonna' is only a translation of 'Mylitta' and of 'Isis.'

Newman said in his 'Apologia pro Vitâ suâ,' p. 195:

'Only this I know full well now, and did not know then, that the Catholic Church allows no image of any sort, material or immaterial, no dogmatic symbol or rite, no sacrament, no saint, not even the Blessed Virgin herself, to come between the soul and its Creator. It is face to face, *solus cum solo*, in all matters between man and his God.'

Where is the unity of doctrine in this declaration of Newman's and that of St. Alphonsus: 'The sentence must pass through this clement Queen, and she well knows how to prevent its execution.'

Surely Newman's head had not been so turned by the 'strength of the logic that had been administered to him' that he was doing the self-same thing that he had condemned in the *British Critic* in 1840, 'attempting to gain converts by unreal representations of its [the Church of Rome's] doctrines'?

Manning's autobiographical note in 1890 continues:

'So also the work of the Holy Ghost, the Sanctifier and the Absolver, with the Sacrament of Penance, enable us to preach and to outpreach all Evangelists, Methodists, and Salvationists that were ever made. Why, then, do we not draw men as Spurgeon,

" General " Booth, or Hugh Price Hughes? I am afraid there are two obvious reasons. We choose our topics unwisely, and are not on fire with the love of God and of souls."[1]

Newman said much the same in a letter to a friend on November 22, 1842 :

'It is not by learned discussions, or acute arguments, or reports of miracles, that the heart of England can be gained. It is by men "approving themselves" like the Apostles "ministers of Christ"' ('Apologia pro Vitâ suâ,' p. 193).

'Why do we not draw men?'

Newman tells us in his 'Lectures on Difficulties,' etc., No. viii., p. 204 :

'The Church aims at three special virtues which reconcile and unite the soul to its Maker—faith, purity, and charity.'

As to 'purity,' we have seen what Pius IX. thought of the clergy, seculars and regulars, in Italy. Are they different elsewhere?

As to 'charity,' we have seen by the quotation from the *Analecta Ecclesiastica* (a review published in Rome and approved and blessed by the Pope) of April, 1895, that it only refers to those of their own communion. Heretics are still to be exterminated, if Rome has the power to accomplish it.

[1] Vol. ii., p. 776.

And lastly as to 'faith.' Newman tells us in his 'Lectures on Difficulties,' etc., ix., p. 223 :

'Protestants consider that faith and love are inseparable ; where there is faith, there they think is love and obedience ; and in proportion to the strength and degree of the former, is the strength and degree of the latter. They do not think the inconsistency possible of really believing without obeying; and where they see disobedience, they cannot imagine the existence of true faith. Catholics on the other hand hold that faith and love, faith and obedience, faith and works, are simply separable, and ordinarily separated in fact; that faith does not imply love, obedience, or works ; that the firmest faith, so as to remove mountains, may exist without love, that is, true faith, as truly faith in the strict sense of the word as the faith of a martyr or doctor.'

That there may be no mistake as to the exact meaning of the 'faith,' we must refer again to Newman's imaginary death-bed scene. There it may be remembered that the Roman Catholic may have blasphemed God, ridiculed the Virgin and Saints, slandered his priest, neglected his Communion, but *provided he has attended Mass, and not denied that he was a Catholic,* he still has ' faith.'

St. James said (ii. 19): 'The devils also believe and tremble.' St. Paul said : 'For the wrath of God is revealed from heaven against all ungodliness and unrighteousness of men, who hold the truth in unrighteousness' (Rom. i. 18).

But what is the Bible definition of true faith?

St. James says (ii. 26): 'For as the body without the spirit [or breath] is dead, so faith without works is dead also.'

At least St. Peter's words should carry conviction to a Roman Catholic:

'And if ye call on the Father, who without respect of persons judgeth according to every man's work, pass the time of your sojourning here in fear: forasmuch as ye know that ye were not redeemed with corruptible things, as silver and gold, from your vain conversation received by tradition from your fathers; but with the precious blood of Christ, as of a lamb without blemish and without spot: who verily was fore-ordained before the foundation of the world, but was manifest in these last times for you, who by Him do believe in God, that raised Him up from the dead, and gave Him glory; that your faith and hope might be in God. Seeing ye have purified your souls in obeying the truth through the Spirit unto unfeigned love of the brethren, see that ye love one another with a pure heart fervently' (1 Pet. i. 17-22).

Our Lord Himself said:

'Ye hypocrites, well did Esaias prophesy of you, saying, This people draweth nigh unto Me with their mouth, and honoureth Me with their lips; but their heart is far from Me. But in vain they do worship Me, teaching for doctrines the commandments of men' (Matt. xv. 7-9).

And Isaiah continued the prophecy:

'Therefore, behold, I will proceed to do a marvellous work among this people, even a marvellous work and a wonder; *for the wisdom of their wise men shall perish, and the understanding of their prudent men shall be hid*' (Isa. xxix. 14).

To quote again Manning's autobiographical note, 1890:

'A third hindrance to the spread of the faith is the reaction against the popular use of the Holy Scriptures —I say reaction because it has been followed and caused by the profane and heretical abuse of the Holy Scriptures by the so-called Protestants.'[1]

Manning would certainly consider the use made of the texts quoted above 'profane and heretical.' Roman Catholics do not have an open Bible, but an expurgated edition annotated by their Church. It is only to be read under supervision, and where Rome has the power, the people are not allowed it at all. Such is the case at present in Peru.

'The leakage in the Church recognised by Manning'[2] was caused by Roman Catholics finding what the real statements of the Bible were on controversial points.

[1] Vol. ii., p. 778.   [2] Vol. ii., p. 592.

To again quote Manning's note:

'A fifth hindrance is what I, for want of a better name, must call sacramentalism. Priests have a danger of becoming Mass-priests or sacrament-mongers.'[1]

'Why cannot we draw the men?' What caused the great 'cleavage' in the Roman Catholic Church in Canada and America? Such an enormous number of Masses were *paid for*, that questions began to be asked as to where all these Masses were said; and then it was discovered that they were performed at half-price by priests on the Continent of Europe. Père Chiniquy has told the whole story.

Newman tells us in his 'Lectures on Difficulties,' etc., ix., p. 235:

'It is not by frames of mind, it is not by emotion, that we must judge of real religion; it is having the will and a heart set towards those things unseen; and though impatience and rudeness are to be subdued, and are faulty even in their minutest exhibitions, yet do not argue from them the absence of faith, nor yet of love or of contrition.'

Then, something more is required for real religion than simple 'faith.' It must be accompanied by 'a will and a heart set towards those things unseen.' How can this doctrine be reconciled with that inculcated in the story of the Roman Catholic death-bed?

[1] Vol. ii., p. 778.

Can they expect to draw the men, if they tell them a death-bed repentance will suffice, and even if put off to the last hour?

On what does the Roman Catholic Church work, except on 'the frames of mind' and on the 'emotions'?

The following appeared in the *Globe*, May 5, 1896:

'A solemn procession paraded the chief streets of Madrid yesterday afternoon. No fewer than 800 priests, with lighted tapers, and thousands of members of religious congregations, also carrying lighted tapers, and 500 sacred banners, took part. All the choristers of the Madrid churches were present, and sang the Litany of the Saints as they marched. The chief feature of the procession was, however, the body of St. Isidro, the patron saint of Madrid, who flourished in the thirteenth century, and whose body, encased in a magnificent silver filigrane urn of the sixteenth century, was carried by priests in a portable altar despite its great weight. The streets were crowded with people, who knelt as the body of the saint passed along. All the balconies were decorated with hangings and thronged with ladies, who threw flowers in the path of the procession. This procession was organized on the initiative of the Queen Regent, for the purpose of imploring Divine intercession for a termination of the terrible drought and a speedy conclusion of the war in Cuba.'

Can they expect to draw the men by this?

What is the cause of the 'cleavage' in the South of Spain? What happened in a large town in the South of Spain at the Easter procession last year? Soldiers had been dressed up as monks, and carried lighted tapers; but they used them as lighters for their cigarettes, and as playful weapons of offence against their friends *en route* who were not kneeling, but standing and jeering.

What takes place in Lima every year? The whole population turns out; the officials of the Government and soldiers take part in the procession, the central figure of which is a guy dressed up to resemble St Peter, and which is escorted to the sea-shore and placed in a boat already prepared for being scuttled. Thus they deal with the 'fisher of men'!

What recently happened in Mexico?

The *New York World* of November 3, 1895, shall answer:

'At a small town named Texacapa ten persons have been burned as heretics by the order of the auxiliary town judge, who claims that he was acting according to the will of God, manifested in a vision. As soon as the news reached Mollango, the principal town in the district, the municipal President and minor officials, with an escort of sixty men armed with rifles, proceeded to Texacapa, where they found everybody in the public square executing grotesque dances around the ruins of the gaol, in honour of the Virgin of Guadeloupe. The judge related the details of his action with great *sang-froid*, and said he was unaware of having done any wrong. He claimed that God had wrought miracles to confirm what a saint had told him in a vision, and had ordered him to execute the heretics. He obeyed the Divine command, he continued, and ordered out the *alguaciles* [constables]. They took the sinners from their beds, and dragged them in the darkness, weeping and wailing, to the gaol. There they were locked in securely, and "I gave orders that the *alguaciles* should set the buildings on fire. The heretics were filled with fear, and shouted for mercy; but Heaven's will had to be done, and they were consumed to the bones, and the vengeance of heaven was averted from our community."'

This man, by Newman's rules, had faith, but it was not of the martyr type; he made others martyrs. Has the Pope condemned this?

In all these cases are the ministers of the Church of Rome 'approving themselves, like the Apostles, ministers of Christ,' which Newman told us was the only way 'to gain the heart of England,' or of men?

Newman, in his Lecture IX. (p. 235), continues:

'You turn away half satisfied, and what do you see? There is a feeble old woman who first genuflects before the Blessed Sacrament, and then steals her neighbour's handkerchief or Prayer-Book, who is intent on his devotions. Here at last, you say, is a thing absolutely indefensible and inexcusable. Doubtless, but what does it prove? Does England bear no thieves? Or do you think this poor creature an unbeliever? Or do you exclaim against Catholicism which has made her so profane? But why? Faith is illuminative, but not operative; it does not force obedience, though it increases responsibility; it heightens guilt, it does not prevent sin; the will is the source of action, not an influence from without, acting mechanically on the feelings. She worships, and she sins; she kneels because she believes, and she steals because she does not love; she may be out of God's peace, she is not altogether out of His sight. You come out again and mix in the idle and dissipated throng, and you fall in with a man in a palmer's dress selling false relics, and a credulous circle of customers buying them, as though they were the supposed French laces and India silks of a pedlar's basket. One simple soul has bought of him a cure for the rheumatism or ague, which might form a case of conscience. It is said to be a relic of St. Cuthbert, but only has virtue at sunrise, and when applied with three crosses to the head, arms, and feet. You pass on, and encounter a rude son of the Church, more like a showman than a religious, recounting to the gaping multitude some tale of a vision of the invisible world, seen by Brother Augustine of the Friar Minors, or by a holy Jesuit preacher, who died in the odour of sanctity, and sending round his bag to collect pence for the souls in purgatory; and of some appearance of our Lady (the like of which has really been before and since), but on no authority except popular report, and in no shape but that which popular caprice has given it. You go forward and you find preparations proceeding for a great pageant or mystery; it is a high festival, and the incorporated trades have each undertaken their special religious celebration. The plumbers and glaziers are to play the Creation; the barbers the Call of Abraham; and at night is to be the grandest performance of all, the Resurrection and Last Judgment, played by carpenters, masons, and blacksmiths. Heaven and hell are represented—saints, devils, and living men; and the *chef d'œuvre* of the exhibition is the display of fireworks to be let off as the *finale*. "How unutterably profane!" again you say. Yes, profane to you, my dear brother—profane to a population which only half believes; not profane to those who believe wholly, who, one and all, have a vision within which corresponds with what they see, which resolves itself into, or rather takes up into itself, the external pageant, whatever be the moral condition of each individual composing the mass. They gaze, and in drinking in the exhibition with their eyes, they are making one continuous and intense act of faith. You turn to go home, and, in your way, pass through a retired quarter of the city. Look up at those sacred windows; they belong to the Convent of the Perpetual Adoration, or to the Poor Clares, or to the Carmelites of the Order of St. Theresa, or to the Nuns of the Visitation. Seclusion, silence, watching, adoration, is their life day and night. The Immaculate Lamb of God is ever before the eyes of the worshippers; or, at least, the invisible mysteries of faith ever stand out, as if in bodily shape, before their mental gaze. Where will you find such a realized heaven upon earth? Yet that very sight has acted otherwise on the mind of a weak sister; and the very keenness of her faith and wild desire of approaching the object of it, has led her to fancy or to feign that she has received that singular favour vouchsafed only to a few elect souls; and she points to God's wounds, as imprinted on her hands, and feet, and side, though she herself has been instrumental in their formation.'

Such is the casuistry of Rome. 'Faith is illuminative, but not operative.' Then St. James, St. Peter and St. Paul are liars.

Our Lord's own words in Matt. xv. 7-9 especially apply to the case of the poor 'feeble old woman.'

Newman did not tell these 'Anglicans' that the Church of Rome, as we have seen, has any number of false relics by which she improves the occasion, and that she has in her pay numerous 'showmen,' who can manufacture miracles when required. The representation of heaven and hell and fireworks would not be called profanity, but would be more correctly described as blasphemy. The story of the nun was left incomplete. Newman should have told us how the 'showmen' priests benefited by the exhibition. Newman believed in the appearance of our Lady, as shown by 'the like of which has really been before and since,' and also in 'that singular favour vouchsafed only to a few elect souls.'

St. Francis of Assisi died in 1226, and St. Bonaventure (in writing his life) says that after his death great multitudes saw the impressions of the sacred wounds of our Saviour in his hands and feet, and further, that there was a nail in each foot, the heads of the nails appearing round and black above the instep of each foot, and the points as if clenched with a hammer underneath each foot.

St. Alphonsus de Liguori declared that during a sermon he saw our Lady 'resembling a girl of fourteen or fifteen years of age, who turned from side to side, as was witnessed by everyone present' ('Lives of Saints whose Canonization took place on Trinity Sunday, May 26, 1839,' p. 12 ; London, 1839).

We remember, too, Manning's story of the nun 'who carried our Saviour in her arms through the convent garden.' But Manning was then an unbeliever. Did he change his opinion afterwards?

'Why do we not draw men?' Because (in Newman's words in the *British Critic*, 1840,) they see Rome's 'agents, smiling and nodding and ducking to attract attention, as gipsies make up to truant boys, holding out tales for the nursery, and pretty pictures, and gilt gingerbread, and physic concealed in jam, and sugar-plums for good children.'

Manning continues in his autobiographical note, 1890:

'A sixth hindrance is, what I may call, officialism, that is, a dependence for our work, not on our fitness, but upon official powers.'[1]

Manning probably recognised his 'fitness' for the position of Papal Secretary of State, and for that of Pope, too, but except in these two appointments 'officialism' had been of enormous benefit to him. This hindrance can otherwise only mean that in his appointments he had not chosen the fittest men.

[1] Vol. ii., p. 782.

CHAPTER XIX.

MANNING'S latest view is expressed in the following:

'I have long thought with fear that the visible Church is now as Jerusalem was in the time of Isaias, and when Titus was round the walls. The Divine Spirit reigns over the "Ecclesia docens et regens," but the human spirit reigns over the Christian society. If this were not so, London could never be as it is at this day. . . . But hypocrisy must always exist till the regeneration of all things, and we must not cease from what is lawful and good, because it is abused by hypocrites.'[1]

The state of Jerusalem in the time of Isaiah is stated in chapter xxviii., verse 7 : ' But they also have erred through wine, and through strong drink are out of the way; the priest and the prophet have erred through strong drink, they are swallowed up of wine, they are out of the way through strong drink; they err

[1] Vol. ii., p. 792.

in vision, they stumble in judgment.' And verses 14, 15 : 'Wherefore hear ye the word of the Lord, ye scornful men, that rule this people which is in Jerusalem. Because ye have said, We have made a covenant with death, and with hell are we at agreement; when the overflowing scourge shall pass through, it shall not come unto us ; for we have made lies our refuge, and under falsehood have we hid ourselves.'

We are left in ignorance as to the cause of this outburst. Perhaps the papers on the Jesuits which Mr. Purcell suppressed, and for which suppression he has since expressed his regret, might have thrown some light on the subject. There is one condemnation of them in these volumes in a letter from Talbot to Manning in March, 1866 :

'The motto of the Jesuits ought to be changed from ' Ad majorem Dei gloriam ' to ' Ad majorem Societatis gloriam.'[1]

Why single out London ? Why not the capital of some Roman Catholic State ? Why not Rome itself when it was still under the jurisdiction of the Pope ?

We must turn again to Newman's 'Lectures on Difficulties,' etc., as he sounds the same note only to a different tune (viii., p. 209):

[1] Vol. ii., p. 388.

'I would say to the world . . . You do your work perhaps in a more business-like way, compared with ourselves, but we are immeasurably more tender, and gentle, and angelic. We come to poor human nature as the angels of God, and you as policemen. Look at your poorhouses, hospitals, lunatic asylums, and prisons; how perfect are their externals! What skill and ingenuity appear in their structure, economy, and administration! They are as decent, and bright, and calm, as what our Lord seems to name them, dead men's sepulchres. Yes, they have all the world can give, all but life; all but a heart.'

It must be doubtful whether the Huguenots and the numerous other victims of the Church of Rome, including those of the Inquisition, regarded her in the light of a 'tender and gentle angel.' The reference to our Lord's words is a true type of Rome's methods.

What our Lord did say was:

'But woe unto you, scribes and Pharisees, hypocrites! for ye shut up the kingdom of heaven against men: for ye neither go in yourselves, neither suffer ye them that are entering to go in. Woe unto you, scribes and Pharisees, hypocrites! for ye devour widows' houses, and for a pretence make long prayer: therefore ye shall receive the greater damnation. Woe unto you, scribes and Pharisees, hypocrites! for ye compass sea and land to make one proselyte, and when he is made, ye make him twofold more the child of hell than yourselves. Woe unto you, scribes and Pharisees, hypocrites! for ye make clean the outside of the cup and of the platter, but within they are full of extortion and excess. Thou blind Pharisee, cleanse first that which is within the cup and platter, that the outside of them may be clean also. Woe unto you, scribes and Pharisees, hypocrites! for ye are like unto whited sepulchres, which indeed appear beautiful outward, but are within full of dead men's bones, and of all uncleanness. Even so ye also outwardly appear righteous unto men, but within ye are full of hypocrisy and iniquity' (Matt. xxiii. 13-15, 25-28).

The 'scribes' were the ultimate authority in all questions of faith and practice among the Jews. Together with the chief priests and elders they formed the judges of the ecclesiastical courts.

The 'Pharisees' were a religious party.

From the context, it is sufficiently plain that no civil institution is alluded to in any way whatever. What has a civil institution to do with 'making long prayers' or 'making proselytes'?

The Pope and his Council claim to speak infallibly in all matters of faith and practice under the Christian law, and the scribes actually held that position under the Jewish polity. The application is sufficiently obvious.

Manning saw it in this light, as plainly appears from

the note last quoted. Newman himself had illustrated the 'outside of the cup and the platter' by the story of the 'feeble old woman.'

We have now completed the story of Manning's life. There is no occasion to draw out in set terms the character of the man. It is not with him as an individual that we have been dealing; it is as an ecclesiastic.

As Newman says:

'How high and imposing do the names sound of Andrewes, Laud, Taylor, Jackson, Pearson, Cosin, and their fellows! I am not speaking against them as individuals, but viewing them as theological authorities' ('Lectures on Difficulties,' etc., vii., p. 186).

It is the system that makes the man; and this applies with equal force to Tractarianism—or its more modern appellation, Ritualism—as to Romanism.

Mr. Purcell's closing words, which may be regarded as Manning's epitaph, are, 'Dead, he yet speaketh.' He speaks to us in these volumes, and that in no uncertain tone. He has portrayed for us in vivid colours the inner working of the Romish system. He has given us an object-lesson in 'Unity,' both as relating to individuals and to doctrine.

Newman, in one of his later lectures (x., p. 267), gave a retrospective view of the Roman Catholic Church:

'Fifty years have passed away . . . and we behold in our degree the issue of what our fathers could but imagine. Great changes surely have been wrought, but not those which they anticipated. The German Emperor has ceased to be; he persecuted the Church, and he has lost his place of pre-eminence. The Gallican Church, too, with its much-prized liberties, and its fostered heresy, was also swept away, and its time-honoured establishment dissolved. Jansenism is no more. The Church lives, the Apostolic See rules. That See has greater acknowledged power in the Church than ever before, and that Church has a wider liberty than she has had since the days of the Apostles. The faith is extending in the great Anglo-Saxon race, its recent enemy, the lord of the world, with a steadiness and energy, which that proud people fears, yet cannot resist. . . . The idea and the genius of Catholicism has triumphed within its own pale with a power and a completeness which the world has never seen before. Never were the whole body of the faithful so united to each other and to their head. Never was there a time when there was less of error, heresy, and schismatical perverseness among them.'

Nearly fifty years have again elapsed since Newman wrote these words, and let us, too, take a retrospect.

In place of the Roman Catholic German Emperor, 'who persecuted the Church,' we have a revived German Empire, with a Protestant at its head. The

Roman Catholic Church has lost its hold on nearly the whole of the French nation. It was recently estimated by a well-known French writer that five-sixths of the inhabitants of France had lapsed into infidelity.

The *Daily Chronicle* of December 20, 1895, states :

'The subject of devil-worship in France is one which in England will provoke a shudder or a smile. The fact, however, that there are now four conventicles in Paris in which the creed and liturgy of the Evil One are set forth cannot fail to interest a curious observer. Two able writers, M. Jules Bois and M. Huysmans, have quite recently unearthed the records of the dreadful Abbé Guibourg's "black" Mass, in which Madame de Montespan was the blasphemous devotee. Dr. G. Legué, in a volume entitled "Médecins et Empoisonneurs au XVIIe Siècle," records beyond all cavil that the "Tout Paris" of a couple of hundred years ago flocked clandestinely to the hideous chapel in the Rue de Beauregard, in which uncleanness and infanticide were raised to the dignity of a new religion. The interest of to-day, however, lies in that end-of-the-century Satanism which baffles all comprehension. M. Jules Bois, with whom I have repeatedly conversed on the subject, makes a point of emphasizing the distinction between the Satanists and Luciferians. The latter take the Spirit of Evil as a rebel deity, and are the adherents of his supposed insurrection against a Supreme Being. They have, it appears, always existed in Paris. The real devil-worshippers are, however, the most typical French sect of these latter days. Their puzzling profanity is now a matter of grave study. Their temples are in the Rue Jacob, the Rue Rochechouart, and within a few yards of the Panthéon. Only the initiated are admitted. The Bishops of Grenoble, Versailles, and Orleans, have thought it necessary to issue pastorals ordering their clergy to guard the tabernacles in their churches from profanation. Not long ago a service of "Reparation" was performed at Notre Dame, because the consecrated Hosts were stolen from a side-chapel. The silver-gilt ciborium in which they were placed was left behind, so it was made clear that the act was not that of a vulgar thief. These hosts are obtained by the feminine Satanists, who take them to the conventicles of the sect, where they are treated in sacrilegious fashion. Those who have witnessed these fiendish functions mention certain phases which even in books on the subject are narrated in Latin footnotes. . . . So far no priest has joined their ranks, and this fact probably accounts for the stealing of consecrated wafers. A Satanist hymn-book has been privately printed, and I may add that surpliced boy choristers assist at the services. The calendar is a blasphemous reversal of the old Christian dates. The great feast of the year is Good Friday.'

Manning himself, as we have already quoted, recognised the 'loss of faith and loss of religion' in Italy. We have given illustrations of the same in Spain. In England the Roman Catholic Church is making no headway, and in Ireland it is losing ground. In the United States of America the Roman Catholics themselves have acknowledged the great 'cleavage.' And it is only in the uncivilized States of South America that it may still be said to hold its own.

That the 'whole body of faithful' are not so 'united to each other and to their head' is sufficiently shown in the volumes we have been reviewing. But, in addition, we have seen the Irish Bishops despising the Pope's authority. We have seen an American Bishop openly flaunting the Pope and his Nuncio. We have seen an Archbishop of Lima outwitting the Papal Nuncio, by causing himself to be named Minister of Justice, and in that capacity freeing himself and his acts from animadversion by that Nuncio.

Canada, too, like ourselves, has an Education Question in hand, and on Sunday, May 17, 1896, a mandate from the Archbishops was read in all the Roman Catholic churches, of which we will quote one sentence :

'A Catholic is not permitted, let him be journalist, elector, candidate, or member, to have two lines of conduct, in a religious point of view, one for private, and one for public life' (*Times*, May 19, 1896).

If this principle applies to the laity, of course it applies in a still greater degree to the clergy. But how is it to be reconciled with the teaching of St. Alphonso de Liguori, or with Manning's habitual practices? Will our Ritualist friends, who before all things consider themselves good Catholics, adopt this principle, and above all will the Bishops of the Church of England declare their one 'line of conduct in a religious point of view,' so that we may no longer hear the cry, so often repeated during the past fifty years: 'I am no party man?'

We are asked to unite with the Roman Catholic Church, in speaking of which Newman, at the close of his 'Lectures on the Difficulties,' etc. (xii., p. 325), could say:

'Yet a little while and the end will come, and all will be made manifest, and error will fail, and truth will prevail. Yet a little while and "the fire shall try every man's work, of what sort it is." May you and I live in this prospect; and may God, and His ever Blessed Mother, and St. Philip, my dear father and master, and the great saints Athanasius and Ambrose, and St. Leo, Pope and confessor, who have brought me thus far, be the hope, and help, and reward of you and me, all through this weary life, and in the day of account, and in glory everlasting.'

We must notice here 'the fire shall try every man's work,' *not every man's 'faith.'*

But what we must chiefly notice is that 'God's Mother, St. Philip, St. Athanasius, St. Ambrose, and Pope Leo' are all coupled with the name of God as the 'hope, help, and reward' in the 'day of account' and in 'glory everlasting.' What is this but Pantheism? How does this agree with *solus cum solo?*

St. Luke, in Acts iv. 12, says: 'Neither is there salvation in any other: for there is none other name under heaven given among men whereby we must be saved.'

Newman's letter to his Bishop in 1841 should be our answer to all such invitations to 'Unity':

'Our business is with ourselves—to make ourselves more holy, more self-denying, more primitive, more worthy of our high calling. To be anxious for a composition of differences is to begin at the end. Political reconciliations are but outward, and hollow, and fallacious. And till Roman Catholics renounce political efforts, and manifest in their public measures the light of holiness and truth, perpetual war is our only prospect' ('Apologia pro Vitâ suâ,' ed. 1890, p. 152).

The composition of differences too must begin at home first. If we cannot agree with our brothers, how can we expect to agree with strangers?

The leaders of the Unity movement in the Church

of England are wishing to take us back to mediæval times. Let us 'make ourselves more primitive.' Let us go back to the Apostles' times. Did they teach the adoration or invocation of the Virgin Mary and saints? Did they wear gorgeous vestments? Did they use incense? Did they practise celibacy? Did they teach the doctrine of purgatory? Did they dispense indulgences? Were Masses or prayers for the dead included in their doctrine? Did they teach that the Virgin Mary was the Mother of God? On the contrary, He called Himself 'Son of man.'

Did they teach the doctrine of her 'Immaculate Conception'?

The Pope wishes for 'Unity,' but he means our part in it to be submission.

Let the Pope first give up all non-Apostolic doctrines, and all childish legends of saints, miracles, and relics, and 'Unity' will be accomplished of itself.

The 'Unity' will be a unity of doctrine. For five hundred years after the death of our Saviour, there was no recognised head of the Church on earth but Christ Himself. There was no precedency among the Apostles, as we have shown, and it was not till Pope Boniface III. assumed that prerogative that any such notion was entertained.

In the Jewish Tabernacle was the seven-branched candlestick, but in the 'Revelation of St. John the Divine' there are seven separate candlesticks.

Messages are sent to seven Churches. But Newman shall answer the question for us in his four sermons preached at St. Mary's, Oxford, in December, 1841:

'The point of these sermons is that, in spite of the rigid character of the Jewish law, the formal and literal force of its precepts, and the manifest schism, and worse than schism, of the Ten Tribes, yet in fact they were still recognised as a people by Divine mercy; that the great prophets Elias and Eliseus were sent to them; and not only so, but were sent to preach to them, and reclaim them, without any intimation that they must be reconciled to the line of David and the Aaronic priesthood, or go up to Jerusalem to worship. They were not in the Church, yet they had the means of grace and the hope of acceptance with their Maker. The application of all this to the Anglican Church was immediate. . . . There was no call at all for an Anglican to leave his Church for Rome, though he did not believe his own to be part of the One Church:—and for this reason, because it was a fact that the kingdom of Israel was cut off from the Temple; and yet its subjects, neither as a mass, nor as individuals, neither the multitude on Mount Carmel, nor the Shunamite and her household, had any command given them, though miracles were displayed before them, to break off from their own people, and to submit themselves to Judah' (Apologia pro Vitâ suâ,' ed. 1890, p. 154).

Newman while he enunciated plain doctrines from the Bible was on a solid foundation, but on writing his 'Apology' the tenets of St. Alphonso are brought into play, and he adds a footnote :

'As I am not writing this controversially, I will only here remark upon this argument, that there is a great difference between a command, which presupposes physical, material, and political conditions, and one which is moral. To go to Jerusalem was a matter of the body, not of the soul.'

Then Elijah, Elisha, and the Old Testament generally, do not enforce the moral conditions of commands. Every Israelite was bound to worship at the Temple once a year. The Ten Tribes broke through this rule, and yet were still recognised, two of the great prophets were sent to them, they were not required to be reconciled to the line of David, and *the Aaronic Priesthood*, nor to go up to Jerusalem.

And Newman calls this 'physical,' 'material,' 'political.' Will the Roman Catholics heed the 'moral'?—

That worship *in any place* of the One True God will be as fully recognised as any act of worship in a temple erected under the auspices of his Holiness the Pope.

THE END.

Elliot Stock, Paternoster Row, London.

BX 4705 .M3 R63 1896 SMC

Roamer, Stanley
Cardinal Manning as
presented in his own
letters and notes
AKH-1924   (aw/sk)

www.ingramcontent.com/pod-product-compliance
Lightning Source LLC
Chambersburg PA
CBHW031337230426
43670CB00006B/354